'I wish that I had pondered  words are a prophetic call i world to pause and re-exam encourage every one of us in the fullness of each mom

Anne Calver, Baptist minister,

IF NOT NOW, WHEN?

FERNANDO DE PAULA

instant
apostle

First published in Great Britain in 2019

Instant Apostle
The Barn
1 Watford House Lane
Watford
Herts
WD17 1BJ

Every effort has been made to seek permission to use copyright material reproduced in this book. The publisher apologises for those cases where permission might not have been sought and, if notified, will formally seek permission at the earliest opportunity.

The views and opinions expressed in this work are those of the author and do not necessarily reflect the views and opinions of the publisher.

Some names have been changed to protect identities.

British Library Cataloguing-in-Publication Data

A catalogue record for this book is available from the British Library

This book and all other Instant Apostle books are available from Instant Apostle:

Website: www.instantapostle.com
E-mail: info@instantapostle.com

ISBN 978-1-909728-99-8

Printed in Great Britain

Contents

Acknowledgements

First of all, I give thanks to God, our Father, who is the author of my day and my life.

In a special way, I want to thank my life companion, who is learning with me how to seize the day – my friend and wife, Andreia, as well as my awesome children, Maressa, Raphael and Grace, who fill me with joy.

Thank you to my dad, Naor, and my mum, Neuza, my brother Naor and my sisters Giselle, Mellina and Nora, and my relatives, for making me who I am and for all the support you give me.

Many thanks to my friend Wilson Suguihara, who was the inspiration behind this book, for my life was changed by yours. May God bless you.

Throughout the journey of publishing this book in English, I had by my side my friend Gary Richardson who prayed, contacted publishers and booked dinners to spread the book idea.

Thank you to my friend Wilson Francelino, who read the book and gave me his opinion; and to my editors Emilio and Rosana in Brazil, who made this book a reality.

I would like to say a immense thank you to my friend Shaun Lambert who opened my horizons, helped me to stand up in life again and gave me a new understanding of how to live in God's presence right now.

A thank you to Nicki Copeland who believed in this project and decided with her team to publish it. Many thanks also to my friend Julian Saunders who gave me a push to publish it in English.

My gratitude also goes to Pastor Luiz and Light of the Nations church, for your prayers and care. You make all the difference in my life and ministry.

Thank you to King's Church Harrow; to David and the eldership, especially Cliff, who was the first person to read and appreciate the book. This has been my church and 'green pastures' for the last decade. Thanks also to London Revival Church, which has been our 'still waters' regarding the Portuguese-speaking Church, especially pastors Paulo and Sonia.

Foreword

Fernando writes from a heart for others, but a heart that is theologically trained, and a mind that draws on the wisdom that God has put in the world as part of common grace.

I have been drawn in to Fernando's story as I've read his book. It is personal but written in a way that we can identify with. I think he has identified a key theme for helping us all experience life in all its fullness, and that is to live in the present moment.

Living in the present is easier said than done! Helpfully, Fernando gives practical ways to do this, with regular reflections and practical and psychologically informed suggestions.

Fernando knows what it is like to struggle, and so writes empathically about our common struggles. A key skill to practise and acquire is gratitude – put simply, gratitude is good for us. When we are grateful, we start to overcome the patterns that culture has formed us in. This is also the graced work of the Holy Spirit in us.

Living appropriately in the present moment also means we are not overcome by memories or traumas from the past. Fernando gives helpful examples of those who have overcome difficulties that are from the past but that overshadow the present.

The book is full of the wisdom of Scripture and helpful biblical references. I particularly like his meditation on 'This is the day that the LORD has made; let us rejoice and be glad in it.'[1] Fernando offers the reader hope, that we can indeed rewrite our past.

As we examine our lives, we can redeem both our present and our past, and move into a more self-aware future where we respond more wisely to life's difficulties. This is an inspiring book and I believe it will be a blessing to many people.

Shaun Lambert, Baptist minister, psychotherapist, and mindfulness researcher

---

[1] Psalm 118:24, NRSV.

Introduction

A Disastrous Start

It was a Tuesday in an ordinary week, in an ordinary month, in an ordinary year.

As we did every day, my wife and I got up to go to work, except that on that particular day she had been moved to a branch office of the company she worked for. It was our plan to go by car to the headquarters of her company, and from there we would take the Underground, and each of us continue to our destinations.

A friend of my wife from work, knowing that she would be going to another location that day, called to tell us that the Underground line that passed near our house and had a stop near the branch office wasn't working. When we heard this, we were pleased that we had made the plan to go by car.

While we were on the way, that same friend called again, this time to tell us that the other Underground line, which we were going to use to get to work, was not working either. We thought about what to do and decided that we could go by car to my wife's office and pay for parking, and from there I would catch a bus to my place of work. I knew I would be late in and, in my haste, I failed to see a pothole in the road and hit it straight on. A little while later I heard an intermittent noise and, using my vast knowledge of cars, I deduced that a tyre had been damaged in some way.

We decided to park the car and go to an Underground stop to catch a taxi. When we got to the stop, there was a taxi waiting, and we asked the driver if it was free. He said it was, so we asked if he could take us to the address where Andreia was going to work that day and, when he answered affirmatively, we got in the car.

No sooner had we stepped into the car than the driver received a call from his boss, and as soon as he hung up he said that he was sorry, but he had made a mistake. He was actually waiting for a group of women who had already reserved the taxi.

We got out of the taxi and thought again about how we would get to work. We walked to the next bus stop and, while we were waiting, I decided to call a taxi company, but the dispatcher told me they had received a lot of calls and that taxis would only be available an hour later. After almost half an hour of waiting, we got on a bus that was more like a can of sardines. After two more stops, the driver announced that he had changed his route because of an accident.

At that point, since the bus was no longer going where we needed it to, we decided to get off and see if we could catch a taxi, but it wasn't possible. So, we continued on in the right direction on foot. We walked three kilometres or so and reached my wife's workplace; she was more than two hours late. From there I caught a bus and finally arrived at work, more or less two and a half hours late.

This disastrous day is part of our history. It's written in our book of memories, and from time to time we think of it and talk about it.

Chapter One

Discovering the Value of a Day

In the introduction, I told the story of a day in which a situation occurred that spun entirely out of our control, a day that was therefore disastrous and quite disturbing to us. At the time we were worried about our jobs, anxious about whether we would get to them or not, and what the consequences would be. At the time, the many emotions this caused provoked several reactions, such as blaming one another. My wife told me that if I had been concentrating while I was driving, none of this would have happened and the car would be working. I said that on that morning I was ready to get on my Underground train, and she asked me to take her to work, so it was her fault, because if she had not asked me to do that I would have arrived at work on time.

And the accusations didn't stop there. We ended up discussing what attitudes we should have assumed regarding the taxi and the bus, and that brought to the surface past offences.

I'm sure you can identify with these things because you must have had a similar experience, maybe even more tragic or comical. We each have our own stories.

Times like these raise a number of questions, but, for me, looking back at the inconveniences we experienced that caused so much stress in our day, the main issue is this: after everything that happened, could we still expect anything good to come out of our day? Could we give it another chance? Could that day end well for us?

We left the house annoyed and we got to work stressed out, but at the end of the day, when it was all over, we started to laugh because, in fact, the day had been a really good one.

So, the question remains: when things happen to us during the day that bother us, what should we do? Throw out the whole day or give it a chance, believing that things can get better? What should we do in regard to our 'now'?

Sometimes we fail to live in the moment because we get stressed about what the future will bring. We are able to play out stressful situations in our heads that cause us great distress, even though they haven't happened. These are the fruit of our imagination and project a future that is still non-existent. I know of people who, for lack of faith in a better future, let their lives come to an end by giving themselves over to addictions or even by attempting suicide. We can also tell actual stories of people who are dying every day because they don't know how to live with day-to-day stresses.

I had, and still have, many difficulties with stress myself. I once participated in organising a conference in London – that was probably one of my highest moments of stress. In the week prior to the event I hosted a Brazilian man called Wilson, who had come to help us and was one of the leaders of the event. He had arrived in advance to help put the last details in place and let us know how the Brazilian members wanted things to be done. Every day I gave him a ride to a particular location, left my car there and caught a bus to work. Trying to get through the A40 towards central London in the morning rush hour with the four lanes completely stopped was awful, so I was always very stressed. So, every day Wilson would look at me and say, 'This is the day that the LORD has made; let us rejoice and be glad in it.'[2] After hearing this for a week and going through all the stress and lost sleep from anxiety and worry, I decided to give some thought to what he had said.

It was out of this desire to learn to appreciate my day that this book was born, and I invite you to put into practice in your own life the principles I share here, because I'm sure that your present and your future can be better for it. On this journey I not only learned that my day depends on how I live my 'today', but I also came to understand that one of the most significant challenges to valuing my present is believing that I have value – now, at this moment. Simply by being ourselves, and for no other reason, we have value and are worthy of recognition. We need to live our lives loving ourselves as we are.

However, we often fail to love ourselves as we are because it seems as though our life is not the way we would like it to be. My question is, 'Who has a perfect life?' And the answer is, 'No one.' But I can certainly say that there

---

[2] Psalm 118:24, NRSV.

are people who have discovered how to live their 'today'. In the process, they have learned that they deserve to love themselves and belong to a group, that they have the right to be loved simply because they are a person. And to be a person is to be the image and likeness of God.[3]

Unfortunately, some people think they need to first meet some prerequisite before they can deserve love – lose weight, have children, get married, be a good father or a good mother, get a 'decent' job, get a college degree, and so forth.

However, I want to tell you that who you are in yourself is enough.

Following this line of thinking, I would like you to put into practice the changes suggested in this book and not be afraid of them. Remember that you are not yet a perfect creature, nor are you a finished work. Rather, you are a unique person who is still a work in progress under the care of the Author of authors, who is still going to complete His masterpiece, which is you.

Reflection Time

- What would your perfect day look like?

- Why do you believe that?

---

[3] See Genesis 1:27.

Chapter Two

Learning to Value the Day

Once I realised that I needed to look at each one of my days in a new way, which would mean changing my habits and upgrading my mindset, I had to make a decision: 'Should I stay in my comfort zone and be this stressed, unhealthy person, or should I embark on a journey in search of this new understanding?' I decided on the latter, and I hope you will too, so I would like to invite you to join me as I share what I learned.

I used to work at the Brazilian Embassy with diplomatic staff that would come to serve for two years in the UK. All of these people, upon arriving in their new country, said that the first month seemed like an eternity, and the first year seemed like it would never end, but that the second year seemed like a racing car, it passed so quickly. I am quite certain that you have experienced this sensation in your own life – of things happening that made your day seem to come to a halt so that you lived that moment intensely and are still able to describe it in detail, as I did in the Introduction. I think that the difference is that there are times when we are able to live in the present with greater fullness than at other times. The times when we are able to live in the present are full, so full that they seem longer and filled with lessons learned, for at those times we are able to pay attention to ourselves and our emotions.

A study was carried out in which some people were trained to pay attention to their emotions for eight to twelve weeks, to try to find out what really mattered to them and how to live in the present every day. The results showed that a person who savours life and pays attention to how they feel has a much better life than someone who is unable to reflect on their experiences.[4]

The goal of this book is to show how we can live every day in its fullness. All of us have the same amount of time for us to use, as we well know. We are all entrusted with 86,400 seconds every day. For me, it is as if I had a bank account and at the beginning of the day someone deposited £86,400, and at the end of the day this money would run out whether I spent it well or poorly or not at all; and I cannot save it for the next day, any more than the Israelites could save the manna.[5]

So, it is my responsibility to think about how to wisely make the best use of this amount; if I should spend it on myself, on my family, building something, working, resting, or if I should just waste it. I am sure that you can find people that use it very wisely; you may find they could be examples that you can mirror in your own life. I am also sure that the Lord can help you with wisdom to do it.

Unfortunately, there are people who waste their day. Some will do it not knowing that they are actually doing it (I have been through that) and others may do it on

---

[4] https://www.nhs.uk/conditions/stress-anxiety-depression/mindfulness/ (accessed 26th October 2018).
[5] See Exodus 16.

purpose. A book like this can be a call to change, so that people may begin to enjoy the thousands of seconds God puts into their account every day. Let's make sure we are not wasting something that is irreplaceable.

I believe that there is a psychological explanation[6] for the time-wasters doing what they do, called psycho-adaptation, which on one hand functions for our good and on the other leaves us dormant throughout life. Psycho-adaptation is our capacity to adapt so that every time we are subjected to the same stimulus, we experience less pleasure or less pain. What does this mean? I will give two simple examples.

If someone falls in love, the first time they hold hands with a girlfriend or boyfriend brings them great pleasure. However, as the relationship develops, holding hands no longer brings the same amount of pleasure. A hug becomes necessary, or a caress of the hair. This need for something more comes from psycho-adaptation.

Similarly, when a martial arts fighter kicks a tree, they may feel violent pain. However, after repeating that action hundreds of times, they no longer feel the same amount of pain, both because the leg gets stronger and the brain becomes psycho-adapted to that stimulus.

In the same way, many of us, over the course of our lives, psycho-adapt ourselves to the day as if we had a bank account with £86,400 in it every morning. For the first few days, we would make a great effort to spend it all, and it would give us great pleasure to be able to shop, travel and see the world, but after a while, we would lose that

---

[6] Augusto Cury, *Think and Make it Happen* (Nashville, TN: Thomas Nelson, 2008).

sensation, and there would be days when we wouldn't even leave the house.

We do the same thing with our days because we live with the expectation that tomorrow we will once again have the same amount of time as today. Having repeatedly lived many days in our lives, we so psycho-adapt ourselves to the days, hours and minutes that it seems that we always have the same work schedule, time with our family and free time, so that based on our usual experience we live with the 'certainty' that tomorrow the same things will repeat themselves. This kind of thinking is totally wrong: it makes us a prisoner of monotony, keeps us in the dungeon of sameness, and numbs us. Instead of living and making the most of the life God has given us, we are overtaken by the machine of time, which does not stop, and we get old without ever having taken the opportunity to live.

At this point let me clarify that psycho-adaptation is neutral and is not responsible for the sameness of our lives, for it acts both positively and negatively. One of the positive ways it works is the incentive it gives us to look for new forms of pleasure and stimuli, such as roller coasters, which are getting faster and with sharper curves all the time, or the sound systems that allow our ears to experience ever greater stimuli. One of its negative effects is when we stop appreciating precious things in our lives simply because we have become used to them – for example, a beautiful sunrise, a pretty flower, or even a new day that comes to us full of potential, with its gift of 86,400 seconds.

Sometimes, in order to value every moment once again, we have to pass through an experience that shows us how important every second really is. Let me illustrate with something that happened that involved my emotions as a Brazilian, as a British citizen (I have dual citizenship), and as a Formula 1 fan.

The Brazilians had not had a Formula 1 winner since Ayrton Senna, who died in 1994, and the British not since 1996 when Damon Hill won. Therefore, both nations wanted it so much to happen again. During the last race of 2008, the Brazilian Grand Prix at the Interlagos race track, two drivers were still competing for the title: Brazilian Felipe Massa, of Ferrari, and Englishman Lewis Hamilton, of McLaren. The Englishman was ahead at a number of points, but there was a good chance that the Brazilian would win the championship.

Felipe started in the pole position and drove a flawless race, but the title seemed far off because, despite that victory, his biggest rival was still in a position that would keep him from winning the title. With only ten laps left to go, it began to rain on some parts of the track. The efficiency of all the cars decreased, and so they began to change tyres. During the final lap the Brazilian crossed the finishing line in first place, and because of the position the Englishman was in, the Brazilian would be the world champion. Massa's family jumped with joy, and everyone hugged each other, feeling that a long-term dream was coming true in front of their whole nation. However, just seconds later the Englishman passed another driver, which gave him the advantage of one more point than the Brazilian. Everything changed. The joy of being the world champion was reduced to being the winner of the race. It was like drinking coffee after eating chocolate; even if it has been sweetened and is delicious, the coffee seems bitter.

On the other hand, the Hamilton family were jumping for joy, and the whole British nation was happy to have an F1 winner after twelve years of waiting.

Taking into consideration, therefore, that every second is very precious, we should take advantage of each one to the fullest. Actually, when I think about seconds and how they pass by so quickly, only one thing goes through my mind: they are part of my life right now and need to be experienced because they make up my day, which is divided into many 'nows' made up of seconds.

I believe that experiencing the 'now' is a lesson that we need to learn in life because, after all, it is the only moment that we can experience. I can't experience the moment that will happen an hour from now or the one that will occur in a little while, just as I cannot experience the moment that happened half an hour ago or even ten minutes ago.

This present moment is like this paragraph: it is not the last paragraph, nor will it be the next one. However, I know that the fact that it exists is based on the fact that other paragraphs that make up its history existed before it, just as I also know that future ones will only come because this one existed. Both the past and the future are valuable, but I can only experience the present.

In this book, we are going to examine the 'now' in our lives and learn how to take the fullest advantage of it, for we cannot live in any moment in its fullness other than this one through which we are passing. The only moment we can live is now. Have you ever thought about how the moment of now that happened a few seconds ago is already past? For example, the spoken word cannot be recalled; it cannot now cease to exist in the past because it has already been spoken; neither can that moment come back so that you can say it in a different way or not say it at all, because the spoken word, just like everything that has happened prior to this present moment, has been trapped in the time that has passed and now belongs to the past. I no longer have the right to change it, nor do I have the power to do so, for it no longer belongs to the moment in which I live, called now. I will, however, most certainly receive the fruits from seeds that were planted, for the past sends to the present everything that was planted in it, both good and bad.

We certainly cannot live in the past, only in the present; and in the same way, we cannot live in the future, not even the next day, because it has not happened yet. Even though we have plans and dreams, these depend on things that are unknown to us. As the Bible shows us, the future belongs to God.[7]

I was born in the countryside, and most of the grain harvested in Brazil is produced in my home area. In order to be able to harvest that grain we have to plant it, water it and take care that no pests attack it. Growing up, it was not difficult for me to understand that in order to have a harvest we had to plant. In the same way, we are today what we planted in the past, so for that reason, the past is important in our life.

---

[7] See Ecclesiastes 3:17.

Likewise, I believe that the future is important in our life. After all, what would become of us if we didn't have hope for tomorrow, or why would we work if we didn't believe that we would live until the end of the month to receive our salary? However, even though I understand that, I have learned that there is only one moment that I experience, and that is the now. As important as my past is, it cannot change my present; even though it has formed me, it has no power to change my now.

My future cannot change my present either, for it has not yet come into existence. Although my present can change the future, the opposite cannot occur.

I believe that the Bible has a lot to say about our present. In various texts, we see that while God provided forgiveness for our past through justification and gave us hope for a splendid future in heaven at His side, He, the marvellous God, wants us to learn to live in the present. Throughout this book, we are going to learn about what God has to say about our present. We are going to see that when the Bible uses the word 'day', it does so in the context of the present and that this is the way God chooses to help us understand that the most important thing we can learn is to value the day.

Reflection Time

You may put a price on your day financially based on how much you earn. One way of doing this is by taking your monthly earnings, multiplying it by twelve and dividing it by 365. It is important to know how much you make, but it is even more important to know not the price but the value of it.

- Could you describe with words, not numbers, the value of the following things? How much is your day worth?

  o Work

  o Family

  o Health

  o Emotions

  o Relationships

  o Spirituality

Chapter Three
Understanding the Present

In the last chapter we began to understand the importance of the present, or rather, the significance of the moment in which we are living, as this is the only moment that we can enjoy and that is also under our control.

The moment in which we live, which is called 'now', is a fact in our life at the exact moment in which we are living.

Some people are not able to look at the present without taking into consideration the past, because for them the only way that the present exists is because they experienced the past. I can understand it, but I could also say that if they had an accident and lost their memory, they would still be able to have a present moment in their lives.

Other people would say that the only reason for the present is to take them to the next moment, which is in the future, but who can be sure that they will live in it?

The way I see it is that the present observes the past and at the same time projects our future. But there is only one moment that we can experience, and that is the present, which is concentrated into our now, which, philosophically, stands still in eternity.

Now is always continuous – it forms itself infinitely – but it is never the same as the past or similar to the future.

The present, then, is the moment we are living in, an eternal present and the only one that we are able to control, by the simple fact of being the only one in which we live entirely.

I think of the story of a boy who was conversing with his grandfather.

'Grandpa, can I live my whole life the right way, without ever making a mistake?'

The grandfather thought about it and answered, 'Unfortunately not, my grandson. The truth is, it's impossible to live a whole life perfectly.'

Then the child asked, 'For one year, then, Grandpa – could I live correctly for a whole year?'

The grandfather spent some more time thinking and answered, 'No, we aren't able to live a whole year without making a mistake.'

Then the child began to ask, 'How about for a month, for a week, or at least for a day?'

The grandfather, after thinking about all the possibilities and considering his own life experience, said, 'My grandson, unfortunately, we can't live for even one day without making a mistake, or for even one hour.'

Heartbroken now to find out that he would not be able to live a life without making a single mistake, the grandson asked the grandfather in a hopeless voice, 'Grandpa, would I be able to live at least one moment without making a mistake, like it was perfect?'

The grandfather pondered the question and answered, 'My grandson, I believe that you can live one moment without making a mistake.'

The grandson left the room, and then returned and said, 'Grandpa, then I am going to live moment by moment.'

That boy discovered that life is made up of a series of moments and days. If this is so, the big lesson is that life is nothing more than a series of the 'nows' (moments) that we experience.

This lesson is great and inspires me to really experience all the moments I have in my life.

I do not know how much you have studied, but I feel that you will agree with me that the best school we can ever be enrolled in is the school of life, which is the school that builds character, and character nurtures human beings who can persevere, who can hope, who can dream and who can positively reflect God.

Therefore, I would say enjoy the moments in life, because one day you will look back and realise they were all you had.

Maybe these moments will be the long walks, or a song played by someone during the rush hour at the train station, or the date nights, or the moments you stopped for a coffee with a friend, or perhaps the moment you held the hand of a loved one in hospital; the real truth is that we do not know beforehand which will be the moments that will always be replayed in our mind, but I am sure they will be better relived if they were fully lived the first time.

So I will again invite you to live every single second of your life knowing of the power of the now, as this single moment can, through a small change or a minor happening, change your whole life.

Live the now as being the most crucial moment in your life, as if it is and will be the only moment you will ever live.

Reflection Time

• How can you live your life based on moments?

• I would suggest you stop and look at your watch for sixty seconds, and see how long it is. (I know you may think a minute goes by so slowly, and it looks like you are wasting time, but it is a valuable lesson of time value and a great experience when learning to live the now.)

• Psalm 90:12 says: 'Teach us to number our days, that we may gain a heart of wisdom.' The Bible teaches us to count our days. Do you count *your* days? If so, how?

Chapter Four

Living in the Now

I hope you are already enjoying your day more, or if you have read up to this point without any breaks, you are beginning to see how transforming it is to understand the reality of God in your now, in this exact moment. When this happens, you can value the day that the Lord made so that you can be glad and rejoice in it. If you would like to know the value of an hour, ask a businessman who, because his flight was one hour late, lost the opportunity to close a significant deal. If you want to know the value of a minute, ask someone who has had a heart attack and was helped in time. If you want to know the value of a second, ask the person who had only a moment to hesitate before turning their car to avoid a collision with a truck that was coming in the opposite direction. And if you want to know the value of a fraction of a second, ask an Olympic swimmer who failed to qualify by six hundredths of a second. These small examples demonstrate once again the value of every moment of our lives and how important it is to make the most of every instant.

We can experience many emotions on the same day, and even in the same hour. We can talk to our boss and find out that we have been promoted – or fired. Or we can find out that the person we are dating wants to be the father or mother of our children – or sadly not. News comes that can change our lives from one hour to the next.

In life we have many experiences which may be either tragic or happy, but I believe that all of them can be used for our growth. As Romans 8:28 says, 'And we know that in all things God works for the good of those who love him, who have been called according to his purpose.' I would like to paraphrase the verse like this: 'Whatever is happening to me right now is somehow working for my good because I love God.' So I know that whatever my circumstances are right now, God is in control and as I surrender my life to Him, I have confidence that He will work them out and bring good from them: 'Consider it pure joy, my brothers and sisters, whenever you face trials of many kinds, because you know that the testing of your faith produces perseverance. Let perseverance finish its work so that you may be mature and complete, not lacking anything.'[8]

I really believe that God can bring good out of what happens to us, but what concerns me is the fact that we can be living an illusion in our minds, so we actually end up not living the reality. That means we can fall into other traps, such as reliving our past or living in anticipation of our future.

An example is a person who does the lottery. As soon as they buy the ticket, they begin to plan what they will do with the money that they haven't yet won. Even though

---

[8] James 1:2-4.

they know that the probability of winning is one in millions, they start to imagine an anticipated reality.

Just as we dream about a shining future, we also love to relive the glories and good times of the past.

What concerns me about reliving the past or imagining the future is that these things aren't real in the present moment. Sometimes when we get out of bed, we are already anxious or worried about things that haven't happened yet. As Mark Twain once said, 'I have been through some terrible things in my life, some of which actually happened.'[9] This saying reminds me of the number of times I have had a discussion with my boss which brought me distress and made me think I could be fired for one reason or another, but this thought never became a reality anywhere apart from in my head. I can also recall many anxious situations regarding my relationships, where I thought that there was no solution and that I should give up on them, but again this reality was only true in my mind.

Also when considering Mark Twain's statement, I believe we can wake up on the morning of our college entrance exams and be extremely anxious because we have studied a lot and we want to see all our years of work pay off. Or we can be anxious because we haven't done anything; we haven't dedicated ourselves to our studies, so we aren't sure if luck will be on our side when we have to just guess the answer to the question in front of us.

---

[9] https://www.businessinsider.com/7-life-changing-lessons-you-can-learn-from-mark-twain-2011-3?IR=T (accessed 5th October 2018).

Indeed, we would all like to know every detail of how our day will be – who we will meet, how each conversation will go, and what would be the best decision to make. But because of this desire to know the future, many people miss the opportunity to make the most of their day and experience it fully. That experience should be an inspiration for poetry, for every day we have the opportunity to make our life a work of art.

Let me hasten to say that I am not against planning for our future, for that would be to go against a fundamental law of nature: everything that is harvested today was planted sometime before. So, everything we are going to reap will have to be planted today. In fact, for us to have a prosperous and fruitful life as the Word of God teaches us to, we have to plant today to reap tomorrow.

We should have hope for a better future for ourselves and for humanity, but I'll keep emphasising that we can only live in today, right now, and we can't depend on the future to make us happy.

So, the Bible clearly tells us that we should live for the day;[10] remember that the words 'day' and 'now' are interchangeable depending on the context. The day is the foundation for our lives, and that cannot be changed. If we don't accept this and instead run ahead to the future or live in the past, we are going to develop a syndrome known as ATS (Accelerated Thoughts Syndrome). Augusto Cury defines this syndrome as the result of 'rapid construction of thoughts, such as worry, the anticipation of future

---

[10] See Matthew 6:34.

situations', as well as 'rumination over past experiences'.[11] He goes on to say that people affected by ATS have the following symptoms: irritability, mood swings, restlessness, frustration intolerance, poor concentration, memory loss, excessive fatigue, non-restorative sleep resulting in tiredness upon waking, and psychosomatic symptoms, such as headaches, muscle aches, hair loss, gastritis and others.[12]

We need to learn to live the now, for this is the time we are conscious of; it is the time that we are definitely breathing life. We can also say that we only connect to God in the now, because that is the only moment we have; in effect, we breathe the very life God breathed into Adam, when He created a new being in His image and likeness.[13]

A few theories and techniques have been proposed for getting rid of ATS. The most common of these are: trying to stop the thoughts, trying to forget, trying to distract yourself or trying to change your mind.

I quite like 'Mindfulness of God', which is the theory that we acknowledge the thought that comes to our mind, and then let it go. For that you should:

- Not overthink it.

- Not try to discover why it came to your mind.

---

[11] Augusto Cury, O Código da Inteligência e a excelência emocional (The Intelligence Code and Emotional Excellence) (Rio de Janeiro, Thomas Nelson, 2010), p79.
[12] Cury, ibid, p82.
[13] See Genesis 2:7.

- Pay attention to whatever you are doing again and let the thought that was disturbing the present go.

- If it is persistent, just write it down, so you can explore it later.[14]

Living in the present is liberating, so liberating that we don't have to live in the shackles of the past or the anxiety of the future.

I want to leave you with a thought to meditate on:

Yesterday is history, tomorrow is a mystery, and today is a gift; that's why they call it the present.[15]

So, open that gift from God that is given to you every morning. You have the opportunity to live your life deeply and thoroughly, but you have to open the present every morning and decide to use it. Your present is no smaller than anyone else's; you do not have one minute less in your day. God has not taken a single millisecond from the privilege you have of living and giving glory and honour to His name. However, it is up to you to open the package, use the present wisely and live your day to the fullest. As the psalmist said, 'This is the day that the LORD has made; let us rejoice and be glad in it.'[16]

I know that sometimes a present comes tightly wrapped and tied up with lots of ribbons, which makes it more difficult to open. So, let's work together to free ourselves

---

14 Based on Shaun Lambert's lectures.
15 http://www.motivational-inspirational-corner.com/getquote.html?authorid=31 (15th October 2018).
16 Psalm 118:24, NRSV.

from the shackles of the past and the grip that fear of the future can have on us, and let us love the day that the Lord has made and given to us as a gift.

Reflection Time

I would like, instead of thinking about some questions, to do an exercise. In this chapter, we have spoken about breathing, and I believe that breath represents life, health and stability and, most of all, represents the Holy Spirit. From the time of the early Christian Church, there has been 'breath prayer'. There are different forms and versions, but try the idea below:

- Taking slow, deep breaths, become aware of the now.

- On your breathing out, choose a word from Scripture, such as 'peace' or 'Jesus'.

- Continue until you feel calm, and know the inner stillness of the presence of God.

- When you finish, breathe out 'thank You, Jesus' or 'Praise God' or 'Amen'.

There are many versions of the breath prayer online and in books.[17]

---

[17] For example, Amy G Oden, *Right Here Right Now* (Nashville, TN: Abingdon Press, 2017); see especially p54. Google 'breath prayer' for an interesting variety of prayers.

Chapter Five

The Challenge of Living in the Present

Living in the present is actually much more challenging than we think. I say this because I experience this battle every day and I expect that you do too. When I read about it for the first time and realised that the Lord was calling me to live one day at a time, to live in the present, I thought at first that it would be a reasonably easy task. But as soon as I started to do it, I found out that it was actually by far the most challenging thing I had ever done.

I realised that many times I would be in one place but would be thinking about another; I would be talking with someone but thinking about my work; I would be in worship at church but thinking about what I would have for lunch after the morning service. I came to realise that most of the time, even though I was in a particular place and time, I was living in an entirely different situation.

Often, we are in one place and situation, but actually in our minds we are living as if we were in another place, in a totally different situation. And even though we aren't really there, just because our thoughts are there, we experience all the same emotions, feelings and anxieties, even though the event is being produced by our brain.

I actually discovered that we live 46.7 per cent of our waking time thinking about something different from what we are doing, according to a Harvard study published by *The Guardian*.[18] I also heard once in a lecture that we actually live just two hours a day in the present moment; at other times we are daydreaming or thinking about something in the past or planning something in the future.

Considering that the only moment we live in is the present moment, if we lived in the present I would say that we could have a better life, a life where we would be more centred, as this would improve attention, reduce stress, improve emotional regulation and impulse control, help with relieving chronic pain, and heighten empathy and compassion; this would enable us to live fully. It might even prolong our lifespans.

Another thing I discovered is that if we are not living in the now, we may not even be conscious of the thoughts our minds generate. The average person thinks around 50,000 thoughts every day. Research suggests that in some people, this number could be even higher, approximately 70,000. That equates to around forty-eight thoughts every minute – without even considering the hours we sleep. The typical person is aware of about 3,000 thoughts per day, so

[18] https://www.theguardian.com/science/2010/nov/11/living-moment-happier (accessed 12th November 2018).

think – on average – 47,000 (or up to 67,000) thoughts which we are *not* conscious of each day.[19]

Knowing these numbers relating to how hard it is to spend my time living in the present and how my thoughts run so fast, the practicalities of living in the moment seem too hard; but I saw that I need to accept and live each day exactly as it comes to me, instead of how I expect it to go. Otherwise, when things don't go my way I get frustrated, and that only results in headaches, wasting the whole day complaining, and forfeiting the opportunity to live happily that day.

How to cope when things are not the way you like? Maybe we have to accept today is the way it is because that is how it has to be. This sounds like fatalism – the idea that fate determines everything – but actually, I don't see it that way. I believe that part of our today is the fruit of our past, over which we had a certain amount of control when it was being lived; by that I mean that in the past we sowed some things that we are harvesting today.

However, not everything that happens in this world is under our control, mainly because we are affected by the people around us, and also by our job, by good or bad circumstances, by incidents that happen to us or around us, and even by accidents and so on.

So then, when I live in my today, many things happen merely as a result of what life has in store for me. I just need to remember that in the end, it is God who allows these things to happen, and what we call 'fate' is in His hands, as we see in Job's life. He lost everything, but God never

---

[19] Colin Symington-Bailey, *What Do You Think?* (CreateSpace Independent Publishing Platform, Kindle edition, 2018), p3.

lost control of his life. Once again, let me make it clear that when I talk about fate, I never remove God's hand or power from being in control. I also believe, however, that this does not prevent me from making a bad decision or from things happening that seem to make no sense.

Look at Job who, after suffering so much, declared that now he had not only heard of God but also that his eyes had seen Him,[20] in addition to receiving twice as much in the way of wealth and blessings as he had had before the hard times came.

I'm also reminded of Caleb, when he said, 'I was forty years old when Moses the servant of the LORD sent me from Kadesh Barnea to explore the land. And I brought him back a report according to my convictions' (Joshua 14:7). Caleb went to spy out the land with the other eleven men, and all of them saw the wonders there and how rich it was; they all saw how large the men were who lived in it, the walls of the cities and the weapons of their inhabitants. However, he and Joshua gave a different report from the others because they did not look at the circumstances. They felt that the land was theirs because that was what the Lord had promised; they knew that if their problem was significant, their God was even more significant.

Caleb believed that mainly because his faith had built a neural pathway that believed that God was able to do everything. I like the NIV translation because it uses the word 'conviction', and conviction means 'a firmly held

---

[20] See Job 42:5.

belief or opinion'.[21] I understand that when you have a conviction you are able to sustain it when adversity comes; it has been built on solid ground – which here is the neural pathway.

Romans 10:17 says that faith comes from hearing the Word of God; it also comes from experiencing His wonders. Here we can see that Caleb must have been listening when he was taught about the power of God. He saw it as the manna was provided. He probably talked about it. He believed it. So, he built a neural pathway strong enough to overcome fear, to overcome adversity.

However, as I mentioned earlier, we do have to face the fact that things happen that are outside our control. Caleb had to live forty years in the desert because of the fear and disobedience of others; that sounds so unfair, doesn't it? But Caleb didn't spend his time complaining about the past or waiting to be happy until the promise was fulfilled, because if he had lived that way, he would not have made the most of his forty years in the desert, or he might even have died of heartbreak. He survived because the neural pathways that he had built sustained him while he lived in the desert for forty years and watched all the people die. Not a single friend of his lived long enough to enter into the land (apart from Joshua), but one thing is certain: he entered into the land, and his destiny was fulfilled, in spite of everything looking like it never would be. I believe that is how it is in our lives as well. Our destiny will be fulfilled, but we have to live today.

---

[21] https://en.oxforddictionaries.com/definition/conviction (accessed 15th October 2018).

I want to invite you to believe that God is the only master of your destiny. He has called you to inherit His kingdom; believe in that.

Reflection Time

The big question for us is to know which path we are building – belief or fear.

- Please reflect on your beliefs regarding the following subjects:

    o Work

    o Emotions

    o Relationships

    o Family

    o Health

    o Spirituality

Chapter Six

Gratitude, a Step Towards Living in the Present

I've already admitted that living in the present is not always easy, but the reason that we are often unhappy has nothing to do with how much money we have, how many friends or children we have, or whether or not we have our dream job.

Here's a big question for us: does our current life correspond with the plans we had for our life at this time? I do coaching. One of my niche areas is with singles, and in my counselling sessions I have met singles who were rich, had a lot of friends, or were adventurous, and while some of them were happy, many of them were not. The reason they were depressed was not because they didn't have money, friends, a house or an excellent relationship with God; it was because their lives did not measure up to what they had planned, dreamed about or put in their life blueprint, which was to have a spouse and children by the age of thirty-five. In some cases, they even had a family, for they were single parents, but without a partner; they had not attained the ideal of a family that they had planned for their lives.

When we are at the stage of burnout, or depressed, it is usually because we fall into one of these classic patterns:

1. We feel like something is missing;

2. We feel that life is presenting us with something over which we have no control;

3. We are focusing on the past and not on the present.

If our life is lacking something or if we don't have control over a certain area, it seems like our present cannot be lived according to our plan, and when our life doesn't go according to plan, it makes us sad and, often, depressed. But if something is missing or we don't have control over something, that doesn't mean that our life is incomplete.

If our life is going according to our plan, according to our dreams, it is much easier for us to live in the present, but if it isn't, it is tough to do so. We usually tend instead to do one of two things. The first is to hide in the past, either because we are proud of it, because it was so brilliant that it casts a shadow on our present, or because we don't believe we are better now than we were then. We see ourselves as people who were worthy of attention only in the past, so we hide in it because we are not happy with who we now are.

Most people, however, don't believe that their past was better; they feel that it is to blame for where they are today. Blaming the past makes us feel better because it enables us to forgive ourselves for our present. We have to place the blame on someone, so we put it on our past. But that solution doesn't last long, and pretty soon we are stressed again with our present situation and blame the past all over again, creating a cycle of negative thinking.

The second thing we tend to do if life is not going according to plan is to hide in the future. In this flight, we run to something that we don't have yet to make us happy. I actually agree with this, as long as believing in the future serves as an inspiration and changes our present, but many people do this not to inspire themselves, but just as an escape. The difference between the two is whether or not this projection of the future changes your today.

How many people say: 'I will have value when I get thin, when I have a house, when I get married, when I find someone who loves me unconditionally, when I am the first in my class, when I get a car as nice as my neighbour's, when I get that promotion' and so forth? The most dangerous thing about this is that these goalposts can be moved. Let's say you want a house, but when you get it, you then want a bigger one, with more rooms; or maybe you want to get married, but after that you are still not fulfilled without kids; or you want to make your first million, but after that you want to make your first ten million and won't be happy because your goal for happiness is changing.

I actually do believe that tomorrow will be better, not because we will have acquired more things, but because I am confident that God is working every day in our lives. He has said that we will grow from 'glory to glory'.[22] So tomorrow I will have more of His glory than I have today. However, I will not wait to be happy tomorrow if He crowns me with glory today, if today He already calls me His child.

---

[22] 2 Corinthians 3:18, KJV.

Many times I have wanted something new, such as the latest technology, and if I didn't get it, I would become unhappy until I came to understand that my heart was hard and I was not grateful for what I had today. It was then that I learned what gratitude meant. After all, how can I be grateful if I am not happy with what I have? The apostle Paul said that he was content in all circumstances.[23] And so it was that I discovered that gratitude is an important step in the direction of happiness. We have to have an attitude of gratitude in every area of our lives and realise that 'in all things God works for the good of those who love him, who have been called according to his purpose'.[24]

So then, let me say again that in order to have a happy life we have to be grateful for the life we have today. There are some people who have very few problems but who live stormy lives, and there are others who have a lot of problems who live as if they were lying in the sun on the beach. The reason for this apparent discrepancy can be found in John Milton's famous saying that our mind can make a heaven out of hell, or a hell out of heaven.[25] That is why we need to learn to live our today, knowing that if it is well lived, it will change our tomorrow.

Author Tommy Newberry, in his book *The 4:8 Principle*,[26] writes that we encounter roadblocks when it

---

[23] See Philippians 4:11.

[24] Romans 8:28.

[25] See John Milton, *Paradise Lost* (New York, Hurd and Houghton, 1869), p10.

[26] Tommy Newberry, *The 4:8 Principle* (Carol Stream, IL: Tyndale House, 2007), p178.

comes to gratitude. According to him, gratitude is as much a skill as it is a feeling; also it is as much a choice as it is a reaction and it is up to us to train ourselves to acquire it.

Nevertheless, there are obstacles that need to be overcome, for they keep us from reaching our potential for joy:

1. Excessive noise – This is the clamouring bombardment of life, the constant connection with people through appointments, emails and telephone calls.

2. Overexposure to the media –Television, social media, the internet or reading the newspaper too much reminds us of everything that is wrong in the world.

3. A 'you owe me' attitude – This is the relatively modern notion that we deserve to get something from other people. 'A proud man is rarely a grateful person because he never feels like he has received everything he deserves' (to paraphrase Henry Ward Beecher).[27]

4. Apprehension or a negative outlook – This obstacle is different from being worried or cautious, which are always followed by productive action. Apprehension involves concentrating on potentially negative outcomes without doing anything about them.

5. Materialism and consumerism – A humorous way to get around this obstacle is to call it the 'never enough syndrome' because, after all, I can always be better and I can always have more.

---

[27] Newberry, *The 4:8 Principle*, p178.

6. A scarcity mentality – This is the very common belief that the pie of abundance only has so many pieces, creating the deep-seated fear that there isn't enough 'good' to go around.

7. Lack of connection and intimacy with God – When you are right with God, you celebrate life in a natural and humble way for what it is: a temporary gift, a treasure with an unknown expiry date.

Writer, researcher, and *New York Times* best-selling author Brené Brown says that we will never be able to live in the moment or feel worthy and deserving unless we have gratitude in our lives. Her famous quote says: 'I don't have to chase extraordinary moments to find happiness – it's right in front of me if I'm paying attention and practicing gratitude.'[28] Therefore, gratitude is the instrument to overcome all the obstacles mentioned earlier and is also one of the ways of being filled by the Holy Spirit.

> Do not get drunk on wine, which leads to debauchery. Instead, be filled with the Spirit, speaking to one another with psalms, hymns, and songs from the Spirit. Sing and make music from your heart to the Lord, *always giving thanks to God the Father for everything, in the name of our Lord Jesus Christ.*
> *Ephesians 5:18-20 (my emphasis)*

---

[28] https://www.goodreads.com/quotes/7167368-i-don-t-have-to-chase-extraordinary-moments-to-find-happiness (accessed 5th November 2018).

So then, be grateful and hold onto the thought that your life today will be better. If you believe that, you will act in such a way as to make it happen. The resulting benefits will reinforce the beliefs you have about your life, which will automatically increase your potential.

Have faith that God can work today; believe, and you will see. Contemplate the wonders of God, His power and His acts every day, and your faith will be increased, and the more your faith increases, the greater will be the move of God in and through your life to bless the people around you.

Reflection Time

- Start a diary where you will write three things to be grateful for every day for a minimum of twenty-one days.

- Please avoid using general gratitude like, 'Thanks for this day; I like my work and my spouse.' Instead have things like, 'My son said he loves me because we went to the park together and he likes it when we spend time together,' or, 'My boss congratulated me today for the deal I have done with this company,' or, 'I am grateful that I could support this person today helping them to be able to operate a computer.'

- You will see how this will upgrade your level of contentment in your life.

Chapter Seven
Finally, the Now

If we live stuck in the past, we won't live today; nor can we live in the present when we spend our time imagining only the future. Just one moment exists for us to live in, and that is the now that can only be lived today.

If we stop to think about it, we live in an eternal present moment. We don't live in the past, which has already gone by, nor in the future, which is still to come, but only in the now, only in this eternal present.

As we seek to live in today, we are confronted with realities that we don't like, but we learn to stop hiding behind worries, traumas, successes or even memories, and to choose instead to be in the centre of our lives and to take control.

Control over our lives cannot happen in the past or in the future, but only in the now, for it is the only thing that exists, and it is only in the now that we can be the masters and shapers of our lives. It is in the now that we can understand that God has a destiny for our lives and that He wants us to reach it, even though in the midst of the journey we often lose faith. '[W]ithout faith it is impossible to please God'[29] or even live in today, for we will be worried about everything, from what we are going to wear to what we are going to eat, as Jesus taught in Matthew 6. We will live in anxiety and worry about a future that we don't even know will happen, and therefore live in a total lack of dependence on God. It is only in the now that we can have faith that God will take care of our today and our tomorrow, which we will only live in when it becomes today, for we won't live in the future until it becomes today. The future belongs to God, as we learn in the book of Proverbs (see 27:1) and in the book of James (4:13-15).

Often, in the midst of a frustrating situation, we let ourselves be governed by what we haven't done. In the past there was a now in which a decision was made that involved a series of issues, whether they were fears or goals, which together constructed a destiny in which we live in the now of today. This will also be lived in the now of the future, although that destiny will be determined in the now of today. So then, there is nothing better than to live the now as someone who knows how to appreciate the present moment, but who also knows that for everything we sow there will be some things to reap today and others tomorrow, when the correct now arrives.

In no way do I want to construct a now that is limited to making the most of today as if there was no tomorrow, because there will be a tomorrow for sure, and we have to plant today in order to reap tomorrow. But both today and tomorrow can only be lived in the eternal now, and this is what we need to cultivate in the best possible way.

---

[29] Hebrews 11:6.

There are times in our lives when everything feels like Good Friday – a day of destruction, of failure. That's what it was like for the disciples when they witnessed the death of their Teacher. On that day everything came to an end, all their dreams were shattered, and everything they had learned, dreamed about and renounced in order to follow Him had been lost. The only option left was to give up, and that is what some of us do in the midst of a storm.

However, there is a Resurrection Sunday – a day of victory, of restoration, the Lord's Day – and on that day every dream is reborn, every battle is revealed as valiant. Every situation shows us that everything we have experienced has served to prepare us for something bigger – even if this experience has been caused by our own disobedience – because it is a lesson learned that could bring us nearer to God. This is true even if it is a sickness, because that would make us surrender our lives to God, and our loved ones would see that only God is the ultimate redeemer.

I exhort you to live the day that is today, to live the now, knowing that God has a plan for your life, and not only will He finish what He has started[30] but He will 'perfect' it.[31] So, live today believing that God's best is happening right now and that it will always happen in your today, for there is nothing better than the now. Even if it seems to be difficult, your Sunday will come and will bring with it glory and splendour, for God takes care of His children and honours them.

---

[30] See Philippians 1:6.
[31] See Psalm 138:8, NKJV.

Reflection Time

'Serenity Prayer' by Reinhold Niebuhr (1892–1971)[32]

God grant me the serenity
to accept the things I cannot change;
courage to change the things I can;
and wisdom to know the difference.

Living one day at a time;
enjoying one moment at a time;
accepting hardships as the pathway to peace;
taking, as He did, this sinful world
as it is, not as I would have it;
trusting that He will make all things right
if I surrender to His Will;
that I may be reasonably happy in this life
and supremely happy with Him
forever in the next.
Amen.

- Please pray that the Lord gives you the wisdom to 'know the difference', as you do this exercise. I have to confess that, for me, understanding the difference has been the hardest part!

- Write down the things you need to accept, even if it is hard to do it.

---

[32] https://www.beliefnet.com/prayers/protestant/addiction/serenity-prayer.aspx (accessed 29th October 2018).

- Write down the things that you need courage to change but you are struggling to do.

- Maybe think about someone who can help you to do this.

Chapter Eight
Leaving the Past Behind

'The sun was just coming up. I got up and made my coffee, and at that moment the telephone rang. It was my mother. As she talked, I could tell that she was sad, and without even knowing why, this made me think of all the family problems I'd had as a child. Just like that, I received that memory into my mind, which opened the door for me to start brooding about my past and determined that it would be an annoying and tiring day.'

These were the words of John, a friend of mine, as he talked to his colleague at lunch about his stress, without going into any more detail. To him, the day seemed more to be endured than lived. His goal was to survive until it was time to go to sleep in the hope that he would forget all about it, and who knows? Maybe he'd have a better day tomorrow.

Those memories were often present in his life, and he wished that he could in some way get his father back for all the problems he had caused everyone. The problem is that this situation had been going on for a long time. His father had given himself over to drink and was extremely sick. During his childhood, John had seen his father come home drunk numerous times and beat his mother and siblings, as well as himself. As the oldest son, he had tried to protect the others, so his beatings had been the most severe.

Time passed, and his life got better. He had a good job and a family who loved him, and he had come to know a God who could do all things. In this new phase of his life, he went to church and had good friends, who always brought him something positive. However, in spite of his life appearing better on the outside, he continued to be tormented by his memories of the past. Whenever they came to mind, he would become enraged and believe that there was no justice here on the earth, and perhaps not in heaven either. So, he would doubt God and his faith would be shaken.

John had learned a lot about God and from God since he had become a Christian. He had built a family and managed to make friends, look to the future and believe that it would be full of good things. Unfortunately, however, he had not dealt with his past. Actually, he spent a lot of time thinking about a better future to avoid the present, which always brought with it memories of the past.

On this particular day, John left work still trying to forget about it, and he decided to go to church. There he heard a message about David, not about his famous battle with Goliath or his reign as king, but about the time he was living in the cave of Adullam, running from his father-in-law who wanted to kill him.[33] The pastor said that the only reason Saul had for persecuting David was the envy he felt

---

[33] See 1 Samuel 22.

towards him. And besides the envy, it seemed that Saul was being influenced by Satan, for he turned away from the ways of the Lord God of Israel. As a result, he frequently acted under the influence of the enemy of our soul, who only wants to 'steal and kill and destroy'.[34]

This was the same way John felt about his father, who had been dominated by the enemy and had given his life to him, so that in time he said only terrible things, stopped working and just drank. Not even the family believed any more that he could change; they were only waiting until he left them through sickness or an accident. They didn't contemplate this with sadness, but they felt as if a great weight would be lifted. The feelings that David must have had were the same as those that John felt: rage, pain, trauma, persecution and frustration, among so many others. Then the preacher pointed out that despite all these feelings, David decided to live his life without dwelling on them, without becoming embittered or bound by the past, but believing instead that vengeance did not belong to him, that he was not the one who should punish Saul. As Paul states: 'Vengeance is mine, I will repay, says the Lord' (Romans 12:19, NRSV). David had two opportunities to kill the king, but if he had killed him, he would have done that which the Lord had forbidden, so he decided it would be better to live as a fugitive than to take vengeance. At that time in his life he was hiding in a cave so as not to be killed by the royal army and, even so, I expect he managed to sleep wonderfully at night, for there is nothing better than a clean, free conscience.

---

[34] John 10:10.

David decided not to walk through the door of vengeance and rage, which makes people build their lives around their obsession to destroy the one who hurt them; their happiness comes to depend on other people or, even worse, on someone else's unhappiness.

This door opens for many of us when we hope that the colleague of ours at work who kept us from getting a promotion gets fired or suffers some personal problem, or that the person who never returned the money we loaned them ends up on the street or becomes a beggar. I know it's quite extreme, but when our hearts are hurt, we wish and sometimes do things that we never thought about before. Vengeance belongs to the Lord, as the Bible tells us in Romans 12:19. But vengeance really enters our minds, and when it does, it feels that it will somehow anaesthetise the pain that we feel.

How many people get into bondage from wanting to take vengeance on their ex-spouse after a separation, or from blaming their parents for their failure to reach their goals because of the pain they suffered during childhood? Like everyone, they have a choice – to stay focused on revenge, which never results in anything good, or choose to make progress in life and consequently enjoy happiness.

Nor is it good to live in resentment, for that also means living your life focused on other people. It has been often said that holding a grudge is like drinking poison and hoping that the other person will die. It will never do you any good, but forgiving and moving on will. I know that forgiveness is not easy to do, but it is a decision. It is a decision that we must make every time the hurt appears, again and again. A proper technique is based on three steps:

1. Acknowledge the pain.

2. Forgive the person and say a little prayer for them.

3. Let the thought go and think about something else.

By doing these three steps, you will avoid living in pain and also letting it dominate your thoughts.

I like to reflect on another episode that happened to David before he became king. During the time that he was hiding from Saul, he put together a small army. He and his men loved Israel, so they protected its borders on one side. At that time, it was quite common for one country to invade the borders of another to ransack it and take its booty.

In time David began to feel that it was only fair that the farmers of that region should help him back. One day he sent some men to the farm of a man named Nabal to ask for food for his army, but Nabal refused to help them. On hearing this, David became angry, gathered his men and set off to take vengeance on the man who didn't appreciate his services.

On the way, he met Abigail, Nabal's wife, who was bringing enough food for all the men in David's army. He still wanted to complete his mission, but she said to him:

> When the LORD has fulfilled for my lord every good thing he promised concerning him and has appointed him ruler over Israel, my lord will not have on his conscience the staggering burden of needless bloodshed or of having avenged

himself. And when the LORD your God has
brought my lord success, remember your
servant.

1 Samuel 25:30-31

David decided to follow the advice of that woman and
did not take revenge, for if anyone is to take revenge for
something, it's God, our righteous judge. Shortly
afterwards, Nabal died. Justice was done by God and not
by David.

I don't mean to imply here that God will kill everyone
who does something to you or that He will do something
terrible to anyone who says something bad about you, for
He has His own way of carrying out justice. Sometimes the
justice tends to take a long time, and we think that God has
forgotten us, but the Bible makes it clear that God gets
angry with those who carry out injustice: 'God is a
righteous judge, a God who displays his wrath every day'
(Psalm 7:11).

David wanted one kind of justice, but God went even
further than what he was planning and longing for, and He
will do the same for you.

David had two different experiences: one that involved
someone anointed by the Lord, in which justice was a long
time coming, and one that involved a disrespectful man, in
which justice was served in a short time. It is the same way
in our lives: some injustices are quickly resolved, while
others take time. In both situations, David was tempted to
make a mistake by trying to avenge himself, but he kept
himself clean, believing that God was in control of
everything, even when it didn't seem like it.

After hearing that message, my friend John began to meditate on the subject, for he was touched by everything he had heard, and when he left the church he took with him a piece of paper on which he had written the words of Psalm 7:11, with this sentence written underneath: 'God knows what you have gone through and He feels your pain every day. He is angry because of it, but His justice will be carried out in His time and not in ours.'

It was then that he realised that there had not been one single day in which God had not been sad because the man that He had created with some love and care had turned from His ways and was now doing evil things to his children.

Stories like John's and David's are unfortunately found in many places, for example, in Nepal, where girls who are only ten years old are sold to houses of prostitution. These girls have no choice, for they live in a culture that is chauvinistic and cruel. If they were to refuse to do what they were asked, they would run the risk of death. However, just as there are people who put them into slavery, there are men and women who recognise the love of God for those children and go there to help teach them and show them that there is a God who loves them.[35]

This God who suffered the death of His Son is concerned about John, the children in Nepal and you, for He is angry every day about the evils of humanity. He is concerned about us when we suffer or are afflicted.

After hearing this sermon, my friend John realised that God has a purpose for his life and that He had allowed

---

[35] See https://www.theappleofgodseyes.com/ (accessed 29th October 2018).

what he had gone through to happen. So, he decided to live in the present, to live for this day in the joy of knowing that God takes care of him all the time. It was a liberation for him that brought him peace and tranquillity.

This is the beauty of the Word of God, which brings liberty to the places where we are in bondage and relief to the situations where we are embittered. It teaches us to forgive in the areas where we are in chains so that now we can live in freedom from our memories.

Our God cares for us every day, every moment, and it is His desire that we are victorious every instant, that we leave our problems in His hands and live out the purposes He has for us.

In order for us to live our day with joy and gladness, we have to leave our past behind, put our fears on our right and our traumas on our left, and look to the future, setting our minds and hearts on Christ and remaining confident that He has much more in store for us.

Perhaps you have already identified something in your past that has you in bondage, or you may find this checklist helpful. You may be stuck in your past if you:[36]

- Set goals but refuse to do anything to reach them.

- Wait until everything is in perfect order before taking a single step.

- Make promises to yourself, God and others, but don't keep them.

---

[36] H Norman Wright, *14 Ways to Make Your Tomorrow Better* (Ada, MI: Revell, 2007), p73. Paraphrased.

- Don't take the steps necessary to avoid physical or moral harm, or even keep yourself in the position of a victim.

- Wait until things become so intolerable that you can't handle them for one more second.

- Allow fear of failure, frustration or change to keep you from taking the risk of changing in order to have a new and better life. Sometimes we don't believe in God and His Word, because He doesn't speak to us the way we expect Him to.

- Are unable to see the various alternatives that exist.

- Feel lost, frustrated, unworthy and hopeless.

- See life through a negative filter and expect the worst in situations and people.

- Underestimate the potential that God has put in you.

- Minimise your situation, condition or problems – in other words, live in denial. I would include in this group anyone who, when looking at the present, feels hindered by something that happened in their past.

If you identified with John's story or with any of these points and you feel stuck and stagnant in your life, the first step I want you to take is to forgive the person who has hurt you. I know it is very hard, for some almost impossible, but we have to do it.

Forgiveness transforms anger and hurt into healing and peace. Forgiveness can help you overcome feelings of depression, anxiety and rage, as well as personal and relational conflicts. It is about making the conscious decision to let go of a grudge with the full support of the Holy Spirit.

I hope that as you continue reading, you will see that the plans of God for your life are for blessing and peace.

Reflection Time

'Forgive' is a word that's thrown around a lot, but how do we actually do this in practice? Dr Everett Worthington offers a practical approach based on five steps:[37]

1. Recall the wound

When we are wounded, we are full of emotions and feelings regarding the situation. If we allow it to stay in us, it becomes anger towards the person who has hurt us. The best way forward is to work on forgiveness. This step is to help us remember the wound as objectively as possible.

2. Understand

At this point, we try to see things from the other person's point of view, so we are doing our best to understand why the person acted the way they did. Moreover, what were their feelings, pressures or agenda when they did it, and how might they justify the harmful acts? Maybe you will just think and review your thoughts, or maybe you will write them down as if you were the other person.

---

[37] See the Happiness Course, Livability, https://livability.org.uk/resources/happiness-course/ (accessed 15th October 2018). Paraphrased.

3. Act

This is the moment to forgive. You will act now, declare forgiveness for the person or people who have hurt you. This moment is a freeing time for the person who commits the hurt, but it is also for you. This step is the crucial one and is made by deliberately forgiving, as Jesus did on the cross – see Luke 23:34.

4. Pledge to forgive

Sometimes we will doubt if we have forgiven the person, as it is always easier to remember the pain. So, in order to make it more tangible, you can write it in your diary or make a 'certificate of forgiveness'.

5. Embrace forgiveness

I remember this happened to me. I took six months to finally be 100 per cent sure about having forgiven someone. I told some friends about it. So, coming back to the tangible, I knew I had done it; therefore I was free from this chain, and I was able to focus on God and what He was going to do, instead of the pain I had suffered.

Chapter Nine

Rewriting the Past

When I think about my past, I remember things that went well, and this gives me the strength to live today, as the Bible tells us in Lamentations 3:21: 'Yet this I call to mind and therefore I have hope'. This should happen quite often in our lives, so we can build good memories and neural pathways that will let us achieve even more.

However, sometimes I remember things that went perfectly, and instead of trying to reproduce them I get stuck in the past, thinking that I could never possibly do that again. Therefore, instead of taking it as a blessing it becomes a curse. It feels like one of those actors who made one successful movie and never managed to get another role! In regard to our lives, the present should always be better than the past, because God is working on us and we are growing from 'glory to glory'.[38]

At other times, I think of things that didn't go well and, when I do so, I use it as an excuse to justify why my dreams have not been fulfilled, or why I'm not living the life I would like to be, and so I feel resigned to it, self-

---

[38] 2 Corinthians 3:18, KJV.

anaesthetised, but the pain always comes back and has to be dealt with.

At still other times I don't want to think about my past, but the people around me do it for me. Usually, this not only affects my mood but throws me into a period of depression, because I was the one responsible for the mistakes and failures they remind me of.

I can't really blame these other people, because they have no idea that they're triggering memories in my mind, which could just as easily be triggered by a landscape, a word, a television show or a thought in the wrong direction.

A memory trigger is anything that opens a specific memory window, whether good or bad. Perhaps the smell of a particular flower might open the window to a good experience, such as the flower you received on the day you got engaged, or it can bring to mind a bad memory, such as the smell of the flowers at a funeral you attended.

What happens is that this reminder causes your memory to open that window which, once it is open, pours into you everything that goes with it. This window is the memory anchor, which is the reading area available to the memory for a particular moment in the life of an individual. So, we can see that when the window opens, everything we have felt that has to do with a person or situation washes over us.

Accordingly, if the flowers were part of something good, they will bring good feelings to us; if they were part of something terrible, they will bring fear and stress. But they don't stop there. According to Augusto Cury,[39] they open the floodgates of automatic flow in our heads. Automatic flow is a phenomenon that is 'responsible for producing a stream of thought and emotions from throughout the history of human life, from childhood to old age, from the time they wake up until they go to sleep at night. It produces thousands of readings in the memory, often randomly'; in other words, automatic flow, once it is activated, begins to produce various uninterrupted thoughts having to do with what was triggered.

I will illustrate with an example. A woman is walking down a street when she sees a store of merchandise for babies. She stops at the door of the shop and begins to hear a mother talking about her son. At that moment she remembers that she won't be able to have a child (up until now this has been the trigger) because her husband has problems with sperm production as he smoked and drank a lot during his adolescence and continued to do so after they got married (now we have the memory anchor). As soon as that window opens, she feels bitterness that she will not be able to fulfil her dream of being a mother and places the blame on her husband, and her world crumbles. From that moment on, absolutely everything is going to be negative, because her thoughts are going to get stuck on that subject (the automatic flow has been activated and won't turn off). From then on, she will remain a prisoner of her emotions and stuck in a past that, although it explains the present, changes nothing about her day.

---

[39] Augusto Cury, *Superando o cárcere da emoção* (Overcoming the Prison of Emotion) (São Paulo: Academia de Inteligência, 2006), p149.

In summary, the trigger is like a spark that enters through a window in our memory (the emotional anchor) and falls into a fireplace full of charcoal ready to catch fire (automatic flow). It will burn for some time until something puts out the fire; normally, when we don't have control over it, only time can put it out.

I think it would be very good if we put it into our heads that, philosophically speaking, it is not possible to destroy the past in order to reconstruct the present, but it is possible to reconstruct the present in order to rewrite the past; in other words, it is up to us to live today, to live in the now, so that our life can be written and rewritten. For if we had the power to erase the past and our memories, what or whom would we erase from our history? Our traumas, our disobedient children, our perfectionist wife who almost drove us crazy, our drunken husband? That's why I believe that God, in His infinite goodness, has protected us by preventing us from erasing our memories, for we could commit a kind of suicide by deleting who we are and returning to the mind we had in the womb, but with a thirty-year-old body. But He also, in His infinite wisdom and love for humanity, has made it possible for us to rewrite our story with His help so that we might live happily in the present.

I know that writing our story isn't easy when we live in a world full of tragedy and sin, but I would like to demonstrate here that it is possible for us to live in the now, and that it is possible for us to live our lives in the present in the presence of the living God.

If we are co-authors of our story, we have to write it in the best way possible, and to do so we need to stop being children and become poets of life so that we can take from our lives the best of everything. Remember that 'in all things God works for the good of those who love him'[40] and that all things were created so that humankind would have control over them, but we lost that control over ourselves.

As co-authors of our lives, we have to learn when to ignite and when to put out the fire of our emotions. In this way, if a spark appears and comes in through the window so that the brain is burning in the fireplace of the automatic flow, it's time that we said that this emotion has no power over us. Instead, we have control over it. To do this, we need to learn to govern ourselves; we need to learn to rewrite the past so we can leave it behind in a positive form, so that when it comes to mind, it can bring joy instead of pain.

So, does it mean that we should never review our past? We have to put our past in order and, after that, leave it behind. But our past can and should be used as a source of inspiration, as Lamentations 3:21 tells us: 'Yet this I call to mind and therefore I have hope'. This being the case, I advise you to look at and relive your memory anchor and experience an automatic flow of positive things that give you hope to live in the present and confidence in the future.

The Bible also tells us what we ought to always have in our minds:

> Finally, brothers and sisters, whatever is true, whatever is noble, whatever is right, whatever is pure, whatever is lovely, whatever is admirable –

---

[40] Romans 8:28.

if anything is excellent or praiseworthy – think about such things.
Philippians 4:8

We have seen that the biblical authors already knew all about automatic flow; that's why they ask us to have good thoughts so that these might characterise our day-to-day thinking and, as a result, the way we think when we are in crisis. They also knew that we should not wallow in our past hurts, but instead bring to mind only the good things in our memory that serve to inspire us and, even then, not in order to experience them again in the present, but only as proof that the God who did something in the past will do something even greater today.

I once had a professor who had in his house a bookshelf where he kept things that reminded him of how faithful God is. God had saved his child from being hit by a car, so he put a toy car on the shelf. Like a good disciple, I decided to imitate him, and I began to buy things to help me remember, but God has delivered me so many times that now I have opted for photos of some and souvenirs of others. The purpose is always to remember how faithful God is. For example, I have a photo in my family album of my motorcycle all smashed up after an accident and photos of me in the hospital. Another thing that I have is the story I told at the beginning of this book, written in the family album to remind us of the deliverance and faithfulness of God on that day, so that whenever we experience any doubt, we can fill our hearts with hope, believing that God is faithful.

God planned our lives to be lived in the present, and whenever we find ourselves in a difficult place we should remember what He has done for us and believe that He who never fails, who has never forgotten us but, on the contrary, has always stayed by our side and promised to be better than an earthly father,[41] the great I AM, the God of the impossible, will once again stay at our side and will lead us to yet another victory over the circumstances through which we are passing.

Certainly, the past should not serve to remind us of defeats or to produce bad thoughts in the present. The past, when it is remembered and relived in the present, should serve to bring hope and confidence in a secure and prosperous present.

Reflection Time

Some people told me that I was useless at public speaking, but that is what I do now for my courses and I also preach in church. So my first thought would be that I am not a good speaker, and the new thought, that I am enabled by the One who inspired me!

In 2 Corinthians 5:17 we read: 'Therefore, if anyone is in Christ, the new creation has come: the old has gone, the new is here!'

• In light of this scripture, what things might you need to rewrite in your life?

---

[41] See Luke 11:11-13.

Chapter Ten

Using the Past as a Springboard

I once watched a movie called *Employee of the Month*,[42] which is the story of a man who works as a janitor in a department store. One day an attractive new employee starts work, and he wants to go out with her. He tries everything in his power to make that happen, but every time he is defeated by his rival. What is interesting is that he is not defeated because the other guy is better but, rather, because he sees himself as a failure as a person. So, every time she looks for something special in him, an extra brilliance, he isn't able to show it to her because he doesn't have it.

We can't give away what we don't have.

As the story develops, it becomes clear that the reason he doesn't have that brilliance is that he has given in to a defeat in his past; his life is stuck in a past experience. The great tragedy is that he has tried to develop a software company on the internet. In the beginning it seemed like a

---

[42] Production company Tapestry Films; distributed by Lionsgate Films. 2006.

great idea, so he invested all his money and also all of his grandmother's (who believed in him) into the business, but unfortunately things didn't go well and he lost all the money. He has had to go live with his grandmother and work to support them both.

That failure had not remained in his past; it is always present in his today. It is so present that he has no desire to try to start a new business or even try for a better position in the company he works for. He has the opportunity to work as a cashier to receive a better salary and a better position in the company, but he doesn't feel he deserves that either.

Fortunately, the majority of people who go through something like this do not attempt suicide, but they do something similar when they go into a deep depression or adopt a defeatist attitude, wasting all their days as if they were killing each one of them. When we throw away our today to avoid the pain of failure, we have actually already declared ourselves to be defeated.

We can see this happen when we have a dream that has not come true, so we deny that we ever had the dream in the first place. In addition to being afraid of trying something new, which for me is the most terrible kind of fear there is, the person can bury themselves further in drugs and alcohol.

Another movie that impressed me was *Rocky Balboa*.[43] The main character, played by Sylvester Stallone, is a retired boxer who owns a restaurant, where he often

---

[43] Production company Metro-Goldwyn-Meyer, Columbia Pictures, Revolution Studios, Chartoff/Winkler Productions; distributed by MGM. 2006.

relives his past. However, his son is ashamed of him and feels humiliated by the bullying he receives because of his father.

At a certain point in the movie, the two get into a fierce argument about life: the son accuses the father and the father says that he loves the son. The son himself is going through a hard time and is feeling finished and destroyed. Then his father tells him that the lesson he had learned in boxing, which applied to everything in life, is that it doesn't matter how many times you fall; what matters is how many times you get up.

Ever since I watched that movie, I have come to call that episode the 'Rocky lesson'. It taught me that it doesn't matter how many times I fall, as long as I am willing to get up and keep on fighting, because it is only in the end that we will know who the winner is.

I don't know which area of your life you feel has completely come to an end, but I would like to share the story of Joseph, which is found in the book of Genesis. I love this because it is the story of a man who took a number of tumbles, one after another, but he kept getting up until his dreams were fulfilled.

It seems to me that Joseph and Rocky Balboa would be great friends. Joseph, a seventeen-year-old boy, was sold by his brothers, which was perhaps the worst of all his betrayals, for it came from people he trusted, from whom it was least expected, and he ended up becoming a slave in Egypt. Probably he could have said at that point that he was defeated and lost, with no future and no self-esteem. However, he saw the situation differently and had the audacity to keep on living, dreaming and maintaining that even though he was a slave in Egypt. In his mind he was slave to no one – not to the betrayal he had suffered or even to his master; he was the master of his future, and he orchestrated his every day by working side by side with the Author, God, as co-author of his own life. He had so much vision that he was put in charge of the entire household of a man named Potiphar, who was actually his owner, but who no longer treated him as a slave. He treated him as a partner, entrusting him with the administration of everything he owned. Potiphar so highly esteemed Joseph that when Joseph was accused of seducing Potiphar's wife, he put him in the prison for elite Egyptians instead of having him killed or even putting him in a jail for slaves.

This happened because Joseph carried himself like a man who was mentally free. What we think determines what we are. The book of Proverbs tells us that 'as he thinks in his heart, so is he' (23:7, NKJV). Joseph thought of himself as a free man who could belong to the Egyptian elite, even though he was a slave.

Once again Joseph was betrayed and persecuted. He could have given up on his dream, changed his personality and lost his faith, but he didn't allow his dream to die or his past to bury him.

Many people give up after one betrayal, but there are some who keep on hoping and believing, and by doing so build a brilliant future in their minds. The Bible tells us to guard our hearts, for our whole life depends on it;[44] therefore, we should use this mental framework to push

---

[44] See Proverbs 4:23.

our hearts, and consequently our lives, in the right direction. Joseph did this and continued to rejoice in every day and sow the good things that were in his heart: seeds of faith watered by the love of God and his hope for a better tomorrow.

Few people would have endured so much betrayal. Joseph had every reason to let his soul become wounded and bitter. After all, he was betrayed by his brothers. He was unjustly accused, but he preferred to be in prison with a clear conscience than to be free and unable to sleep, worrying about the day when someone would discover what he had done with his master's wife, had he accepted her proposition.

His attitude was that of a man who had made the right decision and who could, therefore, be at peace, even if it seemed like everything and everyone was against him. He knew that he was right, and he understood that God was in control of everything and, as a result, he could give thanks to Him in all circumstances, as we are told to do in 1 Thessalonians 5:18.

By holding on to this principle, Joseph avoided falling into a trap with two doors in it, both of which lead to a defeated life bound to the past: the first is to give in to bitterness, self-pity, self-reproach, and a victim mentality; the second is the door of revenge and rage, which leads to an obsession with the downfall and unhappiness of the one who hurt you.

Joseph understood that everything that had happened in his life worked together to make him the man he was when he attained the position of vice-governor of Egypt. His life was an illustration of the words of A W Tozer: 'It is doubtful whether God can bless a man greatly until he has hurt him deeply.'[45]

So, Joseph decided that even though he was in prison he would do his best, and he was put in charge of all the other prisoners, just because he lived in the hope of a better day, did not allow the past or the future to control his life, and carried out his daily tasks with joy.

And because he was able to free himself from the past, forgive and live for the present, when he was reunited with his brothers and found out that his family needed help, he provided them with food, revealed himself to them and invited them (including the brothers who had betrayed him) to come to live in Egypt. His forgiveness was so complete that he never took revenge on his brothers, not even after the death of their father, because he understood that God had everything under His control.

That's the beauty of the Word of God, which sets us free where we were in bondage, gives us relief where we were embittered, and teaches us to forgive where we were in shackles. It is how we can be set free from sad reminders of the past.

Another thing that the Bible teaches us about the past is in Lamentations 3:21, which says that we should bring to mind that which gives us hope. Many people, when they get depressed, keep their heads down, their shoulders stooped, and their bodies slumped, reminding themselves of everything that's bad. Others, like Joseph, take the opportunity to believe in a God who cares for them, in a God who controls history, and in that way change their

---

[45] A W Tozer, *The Root of the Righteous* (Chicago, IL: Moody Publishers, 2015), p165, Kindle edition.

thinking and their posture and bring to mind things that can give hope. You do that by following the advice given by Paul in 2 Corinthians 10:5 – bringing 'every thought captive'[46] – so you choose to think like God thinks. You base your thinking on the right principles, which will give you the best results.

I'm old enough to recognise that I've done many things wrong. I've repented of lots of things that I have done, and I want very much for my life to be different in some areas, so sometimes I have a pity party.

Maybe you've never done that, but I have a tendency to. I can waste three days watching television to forget my problems, as if everything will go away if I make no decisions at all. Unfortunately, nothing happens until I take responsibility, change my thinking and begin to live again and, instead of reminding myself of the terrible past, exchange the picture I have in my head for one that promotes an enjoyable present and a better future. Our God takes care of you every day and every moment, and it is His desire that we are victorious every instant, that we leave our problems in His hands and live out what He has for us. God's heart is so deep that we can trust Him with everything and He will do the rest.

If we are going to live today with joy and gladness, we have to put our lousy past behind us, our fears on our right-hand side and our traumas on the left-hand side, and look straight ahead, placing our minds and hearts in Christ and being confident that He has much more in store for us. God's best will come to us as we live the fullness of now,

---

[46] NRSV.

of today, in all things, and if we remember the past, remind ourselves of the good things that give us hope and put a smile on our face.

Reflection Time

- Write down the things that are still bothering you, everything that upsets you, on a piece of paper.

- Read what you have written out loud.

- What have you learned from reading this list back to yourself? Note any thoughts.

I believe that by now you are able to perceive that your mind can be in control of your thoughts, and not the other way around. But if your thoughts are still disturbing you, it is time to put them at the foot of the cross and ask God for His divine exchange, so that you may rewrite your thoughts and use them as a springboard for God's glory. You will then be blessed by exchanging your load for His, letting go of all your hurt, and choosing to forgive and move on from everything that is holding you down.

Chapter Eleven

Using the Past to Bless the Present

Learning to live today and leave the past behind has been the topic of the last three chapters. We have learned to look at the past as something that is behind us, in the sense that we can no longer live in it, while at the same time recognising the necessity of taking responsibility for our lives to create an enjoyable present and a better future. We saw this in the life of Joseph, who by doing these things made himself more than a conqueror[47] in God.

There is no denying that the past formed our present; it was in the past that we wrote the earlier pages of our lives. So, we cannot minimise the importance of the past; on the contrary, I believe that the past, when utilised properly, can serve as a tool to help us understand the present and build a more relevant future. Our lives are a story made up of various chapters that are narratives unique to our lives.

Narratives are the best way to interact with the lives of others, including our own; that's why television dramas are so successful. When we look at the most powerful and

---

[47] See Romans 8:37.

widely read book in the world, the Bible, we notice that it is mostly made up of narratives that tell the story of faith; the Old Testament almost entirely consists of narratives, as do the first five books of the New Testament, which include the life of Jesus.

I have also noticed that the best way to give a testimony is to tell the story of what Christ has done in my life, for no one can deny or contest that story, because it is my story.

So then, when I look back at my story, I see that much of what has taken place in my life is the fruit of something that has happened in the past. That doesn't make me relive my past; it helps me better understand my present and plan my today in such a way that it will lead to a better present in the future.

Understanding my past helps me bring to mind things that can give me hope, as well as helping me put traumas behind me and showing me my potential in a given direction. That being the case, it helps me in my today to know what direction to take in light of what I have learned.

I have learned that my life can be enhanced to the degree that my story is told. And depending on how I rewrite my story, I see that nothing has happened by accident.

When I read my life, I see that:

1. God is not only the Creator of my life. He is much more than that, for He is the author who wrote my past and is still writing my present and will write my future. In that way, He will use the story of my life to reveal something about Himself.

2. When I look at my story, I see that my life is not a montage of random scenes, like a string of television

commercials that have nothing to do with each other, but rather it is like a television show in which all the scenes have connections between them.

3. When I understand the story of my life, admit my mistakes and successes, and take responsibility for who I am, then I can work together with God as co-author of my life.

4. And when I understand that God is authoring my life to reveal His image on the earth and that He has given me the opportunity to co-author with Him every scene of my life, then I can share my own story with the world to bless those who hear it.

As we have seen, our story is full of good, happy days, as well as days that are full of difficulties and problems. However, I want to tell you that our God can turn those days of trauma and great pain into days of joy.

In Joel 2:25 the Bible states that God was going to restore to the people of Israel the years that the enemy had stolen from them, which the locusts had destroyed. God did this many times, and many people gained more in the end than they had previously. We can point to Job, who received twice as much as he had, but what Job talked about the most was that he had learned about God in the process.

A modern example that I especially like is the life of Joyce Meyer. The short version of her story is that she was sexually abused by her father, and the terror she lived through created trauma in her life. Now she has an international ministry, and what she says about her life is that God used everything in her past to make her who she is today and that God restored all things and gave her even more than she deserved.[48]

What we learn from the stories of Job and Joyce Meyer is that God does not keep us from the day of adversity; these days happen because we live in a fallen world.[49] This being the case, we go through periods in which we alternate between certainty that something will happen in our lives and doubt. It's the fruit of a 'normal' caused by the anomaly of sin that has taken creation from the security and certainty of the Garden of Eden to the uncertainty and tension of the world as it is now. However, Job and Joyce also remind us that just as God turns weeping into joy, so He uses 'all things … for the good of those who love him',[50] and their stories are examples of how He, through His sons and daughters, blesses the world. Job and Joyce remind us that God uses people with the same backgrounds that we have. He uses whomever He wants to, whatever their past, and He uses us because of our past as well.

Life is like a movie. Like life, the film begins calmly until something happens and turns everything upside down, bringing tension and adversity. Once this abnormality has occurred, we spend the rest of the movie in search of the resolution that will bring everything back to normal and perfect peace.

It is as if we were watching a movie in which, during the first ten minutes, we see a perfect family, and then a kidnapping happens. For the rest of the film the people

---

[48] https://abcnews.go.com/Nightline/joyce-meyer-transparent-evangelist/story?id=10355887 (accessed 29th October 2018).
[49] See Genesis 3.
[50] Romans 8:28.

involved try to solve the problem and, usually, the person is rescued when things are at their worst, and in a most surprising way.

We see this scenario played out in Joyce Meyer's life. I would like to show you how it has worked in my own life as well.

I was the last one of all my closest friends to get married. For a long time, I didn't think much about marriage, but the world around me began to make me feel like I wasn't following the pattern. After all, according to them, how could a good-looking, intelligent, caring young man not be married?!

Besides my family and friends, the church seemed to have closed its doors on me as well. I already had friends who had left the church because they couldn't find a place where they fitted as single people over thirty.

This situation began to really bother me, so I started to study the topic. Seven years later I finished a book that told my story in light of biblical principles and sociology, called *Single, in a Married Church?*[51] Through the book, I was able to share my story with others who were dealing with the same issues and who were looking for someone like me to share my experiences and give them hope for the future.

This kind of sharing is critical, because we tend to suffer from what I call 'the Elijah syndrome'. The prophet Elijah (in 1 Kings 19) was in fear of his life, because Jezebel, queen of Israel, was looking for him to kill him. In his fear he runs away and afterwards, exhausted and sitting under a tree, he asks God to kill him.

---

[51] Fernando De Paula, *Solteiro, numa igreja casada?* (Single, in a Married Church?) (Sao Paulo: Folego, 2012).

God, in His infinite goodness, asks what the matter is, and Elijah answers, 'I have been very zealous for the LORD God Almighty. The Israelites have rejected your covenant, torn down your altars, and put your prophets to death with the sword. I am the only one left, and now they are trying to kill me too' (1 Kings 19:10).

Actually, this wasn't true; God had many other prophets in hiding. The way the Elijah syndrome works is that when we have a problem, we think we are the only ones who have that problem, who have ever had it or ever will, so that no one else could possibly understand, let alone help us. However, that is not the case. Even though none of us experiences the same things in exactly the same way, because we are all unique, there are other people who have gone through or are going through something very similar to what we are experiencing. We can be certain, therefore, that we can find someone to help us when we are having a hard time, just as we can be sure that we will be able to help someone else in the future.

In my case, after going through this trauma, I decided to take responsibility for myself, and I came to realise that God's love in my life did not depend on my marital status. It relies only on the love He has for me. As a result of this personal growth, I felt that I should share with others who were going through the same thing so that they could be helped. I invite you to share your own life story as well.

Maybe you've noticed that directors of orphanages are often former orphans, or that the leaders of organisations to protect women and children from domestic violence were themselves victims of it.

We are never far away from someone who has issues, as we know that in every family there may be someone who was unfaithful, a cousin who drinks too much, an eccentric aunt, a homeless brother or gossipy sisters, not to mention disreputable parents.

In order to try to find out more about myself, I looked to my past and saw some big and also some small points, moments and occasions that helped to shape me into who I am. These are the parts of my story that can help others.

I'm sure you also have things in your story that would bless others if you talked about them, and I encourage you to do just that.

First of all, for this to happen you need to write down your story – not to get stuck in those things, but to get free from your past and discover your life passion.

For some time, I wrote my story during my lunch hour. This was after I married. As I wrote, I began to see problems that needed to be resolved and passions that seemed to have been sidelined. I remember the day I was suddenly able to see that because I had had a lot of women around me (three older sisters and my mother), I did everything I could to get them to accept me and that I was doing the same thing now with my wife. It also became clear to me that I had squashed my own identity in the process, which was why it caused me so much pain. My wife had never asked me to do this; it came out of my history. I believe that now we are much healthier in this area, without having made any major changes in our lifestyle. It happened as the result of me finding balance inside myself. I still bring her coffee in bed and support her in every way I can, but now I realise that I have my own passions and desires as well.

During the exercise of writing my story, I also rediscovered my passion for the youth in the church. I had worked my whole life with youth, and I decided I needed to get back to that kind of ministry. We prayed and now, in addition to our other activities, we are having young people over to our house and sharing the Word of God with them and discussing their plans and dreams.

Looking at my passion, I found that it was closely tied to my own suffering and disillusionment. When I studied the root of the word 'passion', I discovered that the Latin root means 'to suffer or endure a difficult situation', which seems to indicate that when we fall in love, either we will do so because we are suffering, or we are going to hurt for the person with whom we are in love.

When we discover our passion, we are also exploring the desire of God's heart for our lives.

I remember visiting a missionary who works with fishermen, and he said, 'Many people think that the life we live is difficult and that we're suffering here because of our arduous mission, but actually we are here because God put the desire to come here in our hearts. He put this passion in our hearts. That's not to say that the work doesn't demand a lot of effort on our part, but there is nothing else that would give us more pleasure and fulfilment than to work with these fishermen and spend half of our time on boats. Our passion put us inside the desire of God's heart because it was He who motivated it, so our passion is nothing more than the will of the author of our lives inside of us.'

I invite you to write your story and look at both the happy times and the difficult ones. Don't know how to write? Don't write anything down; just wait a bit, and the thoughts will begin to come. Don't question them – just write them down, and with time you will see that everything you have written was for a reason.

With some analysis and prayer, dedicating it to the Lord, your life story will be a blessing for many people. Remember that the reason for writing down the past is to liberate your present, because it is through our history that we can understand who we really are and we can discover the ideal person we want to become.

Did you know that the decisions we make are based much more on who we think we are than who we really are? To define who we are is actually nearly impossible, but it isn't difficult to identify what our ideal is, because that's what we base our decisions on. Our ideal will also reveal to us what we value (our passion), how we see the world (our beliefs) and what we need to do to reach our ideal (our behaviour).

When you discover your passion, you will find that it leads you to choose one path over others, a path that will be as unique as your fingerprints.

I don't know what your passion is, and maybe you don't either, so I will close this chapter by challenging you to find it. It will be revealed by studying your past and will bring with it an understanding of today and help in making decisions for the future.

Reflection Time

- What is my passion? What do I enjoy doing?

- How is my passion linked to my past?

- How can I connect my past and my passion to bless people around me?

Chapter Twelve
Let the Future Be the Future

Another sunny day on the beach at Itapuã, in the northern part of Brazil. A small family, made up of a mother and two children aged six and eight, are taking advantage of it to get a tan, play in the sand and spend their summer vacation together. They are sharing special moments together that will have a lasting effect on all of them, except for the father, who has had to miss yet another trip because of work.

Far from his family and missing them terribly, he talks with the children on his mobile phone and is happy that they are making the most of their school holidays. At their mother's request, they tell him that he is a great dad, and the older one adds that she is dying to see him again since they have already spent two weeks without him.

The father hangs up the phone and returns to his computer to bring his work up to date. As he begins to type, he thinks about the family time that he is missing and begins to wonder if everything he is doing is worth it. Just to be sure, he writes a short autobiography to convince himself that he is on the right path for his life and his family.

Sérgio, that man who works a lot and is missing his family, took night classes to get a degree in business administration because he had to work during the day to pay his tuition fees. In spite of these challenges, he graduated with honours. Now he is in charge of the sales department in an up-and-coming company and is hoping to be promoted to the regional office because from there he is sure that in a short time he will become a director of the company. Through his marketing techniques, sales have skyrocketed and his materials are being reproduced and used by all the regional offices. In the euphoria of everything going so well, he is already dreaming of getting an MBA[52] in the United States, so he is studying English.

Having come from a middle-class family that had never managed to own anything, he had grown up in a rented house. At this point in his life, he already feels like he has made it because he has taken out a mortgage on an apartment and only has one year left to pay on it. He has married a pretty woman and has two children of whom he is very proud because they do well in school. The older daughter takes ballet classes and the younger son studies the viola, and both of them say that they want to be like their father professionally.

In order to do all this and provide a good life for his family, he has decided to work long hours every day in the office as well as more hours from home, so he usually doesn't travel with the family. He can't afford that luxury because he always has a new strategy to plan, a new administrative structure, a new team, a new development

---

[52] Master of Business Administration.

meeting. Actually, all he thinks about is the business and his career.

There is not only the external competition; there are also internal disputes over promotion, for there are others inside the company who also want to be promoted and have good ideas, so he has to be even more careful to make sure that his bosses are always aware of the results he is bringing to the company.

Reassured once again that he is doing the right thing for his family, he turns his thoughts back to the various plans he has for the new products the company is developing.

It's nine o'clock at night, and he decides to watch a television programme about people striving to be successful in the business world.

After watching the programme, he returns to the computer and sees the photos of his family on the screen. Suddenly he stops, bursts into tears and begins to think: what's the advantage of having two new cars in the garage, an apartment that is almost paid off, many miles of travel, and a family that he never sees?

He has everything he'd ever dreamed of and the possibility of obtaining even more, but he has not fulfilled his personal dreams, because he has no time to play with his children or travel with the family, have cookouts at the weekend or play ball with his friends. Everything he is doing is for acquisition, not fulfilment. He is working to ensure a secure future when he retires, but he is not living in today.

How many of us spend our days building a future and security for when we are older, but waste all the strength of youth, lose our hair sooner and end up with lots of wrinkles? Thinking only of the future, we work like crazy and once again miss our chance to live today, to enjoy the fulfilment of a sunny morning or a clear, starry night, all in order to attain more than we need or store up wealth for the future. We mistakenly think that we can control the future and that today is not relevant.

In our anxiety to make sure that the future is secure, we forget about today, but the only moment that we can actually live is right now. We don't live in the past, although we are affected by it, nor do we live in the future, for it doesn't belong to us, simply because it does not exist.

This is not to say that we shouldn't plan for the future, because that would be to tell you that you can't have dreams. If I were to say to a farmer not to plant since he can't trust in the future, he would tell me, 'How am I going to harvest anything tomorrow if I don't plant today? How am I going to reap six months from now if I don't sow today? Whether the future is uncertain or not, I have to plant today, because that is a law of nature that cannot be broken. If I don't, we'll have no way to stay alive in the future, for lack of food.'

In Sérgio's case, he is more concerned about how he is going to live tomorrow than he is about his career and family. Many of us are sure that when we have enough money to live for the rest of our lives, everything will be fine. Others think that if they have enough money to pay any doctor or medical plan for the rest of their lives, they won't die from sickness of any kind, and this is comforting.

The way I see it, the problem is not with money in itself; it is believing that money will bring the happiness and security that the soul needs so much. However, what the soul really needs is not financial security, but the security that comes from God.

Jesus told a story, recorded in Luke 12:13-21, about a man who had such a great harvest that he stored up his riches and felt like he was set for the rest of his life, but who forgot to protect his soul, to put his life in the hands of God. That man never thought about eternity, nor was he content to live in the present; instead, he tried to guarantee his ability to rest, drink, eat and be merry in the future.

Every day I eat, drink and enjoy myself, and that is because I have learned that I do not depend on money or the future; I depend on the Lord, and I believe in Psalm 118:24: 'This is the day that the LORD has made; let us rejoice and be glad in it.'[53] A few years ago, I participated in a workshop at which the speaker made the statement, 'I would rather my son be a street sweeper and love the Lord than a millionaire who does not know God.' A lady interrupted him and said, 'But your children are at university. How can you say that, when you are investing in them?' The speaker answered, 'I want my children to be successful professionally, but I always tell them: don't let go of your principles in order to have money or success in your profession. Always make every effort to have a better future, but never, never let go of God's hand, for what advantage is it to gain the whole world and lose Christ?'

One day I was talking with a friend who was very successful, but who only went to church once every two months – partly owing to lack of commitment and partly because of his many business trips – and whose children

---

[53] NRSV.

were far from God. I told him that I would prefer that my daughter, who was four months old at the time, clean houses for a living than be far from the Lord. He looked at me with surprise and ever since he has teased me, 'How's the cleaning girl in your house doing?' At the time, the joke bothered me because I want very much for my daughter to be successful, and I had only said that to him to make the point that God is more important than professional success. So I prayed, 'I want very much for my daughter to be successful in life, Lord, but no matter how we define success, I believe that this can only happen if she does the most important thing in her life, which is to love You and worship You, for I believe that once she takes that first step, everything else that You have for her will be added, as the Scripture says in Matthew 6:33.'

I think that many people hope that their future will be filled with money and good things, so they end up forgetting to live every day that the Lord has made and miss the opportunity to be happy now in order to invest in an uncertain future.

In response to this, I would like to take the next few chapters to reflect on how our future is not in our hands, except to the extent that we can sow today in order to reap a future 'now' that is much better.

Reflection Time

- How do we deal with the anxiety of something that has not yet happened?

- Some of us try to stop worrying about the future, but end up having more trouble, because when we try to ignore it, we end up thinking about it. Like if I say to you: 'Do not think about a pink elephant.' You probably just did it.

- One way of letting go and letting the future be the future is to acknowledge the anxiety and release it.

- You may find it helpful to use the 'breath prayer' we mentioned earlier. Practising Christian mindfulness may be useful. You could take the four steps proposed by Amy G Oden in her book *Right Here Right Now*.[54]

- Christian mindfulness is something that you can do any time and anywhere, because you have everything you need to get started: your breath, your body and God's presence.

Try the following steps:

1. Attention to your breathing (thirty seconds)

Start to space your breaths, maybe counting up to four when breathing in and up to seven when breathing out. As you do it, you will notice your breathing; you will also start to feel your lungs and diaphragm rise and fall, and will have the sensation of the air through your nose. Keep doing it purposefully, and fully experience it. Remember that life started like that when God breathed on us. Since then we have the gift of breathing without stopping, as the

---

[54] Oden, *Right Here Right Now*. Paraphrased.

body does that for us, but we can also choose to do it mindfully and attentively.

2. Listen to your body (thirty seconds)

Keep doing this attentively and let your breathing fill not just your lungs but your whole body. Remember that the oxygen goes through your entire body, so visualise it filling your lungs, expanding to your arms and legs, then your hands and feet, and on to your brain, providing life-giving oxygen throughout your body. Please note the sensation or feeling, maybe a tingle here or a tightness there. Remember that this is a noticing process, not an analysing or justifying one, so observe it. According to the Bible, the body is the temple of the Holy Spirit, so is blessed and part of our worship to God, as described in Romans 12. So, to use your body to connect yourself to God is definitely a proper use of it, and it is also part of our worship to a God who is able to meet us in our bodies, right here and right now.

3. Acknowledgement (thirty seconds)

A lot of things like feelings, thoughts, sensations and attitudes could be coming to your mind right now, so it is time to acknowledge them as you continue to breathe and embody the air flow.

This is the time to stop judging and just observe, as this space gives you a chance to actually know what is happening in your body. So acknowledge thoughts as if they were a train passing by; don't stop the train or rifle through its cargo.

This step is like calling you to sit on a rock on the top of a hill, so you can look at your life as the train passing by, seeing all the feelings and thoughts as carriages, which means that each of them is part of the train and not the full train. At this moment we can stop the cycle of reactivity that often drives our behaviour and see that we have control of it.

So we do not need to accept any prejudicial thought, as we can control it. But this time of acknowledgement is an excellent opportunity to put it before the Lord as a prayer.

At this moment we can work out our feelings, thoughts, sensations and attitudes as we prayerfully bring them before the Lord, as we are open to listening to His voice more than speaking. So at this time, the Lord is able to work in our lives in surprising ways as we stop trying to excuse or justify ourselves. We can acknowledge that the Lord is sharing with us whatever we are going through.

This is also a great time to imagine Jesus by your side, healing any hurt or expanding any blessing. Because He loves you.

4. Encounter (thirty seconds)

As you acknowledge whatever arises in the presence of Jesus, pay attention to the new shapes of your feelings, thoughts, sensations and attitudes. I hope you feel the healing power of Jesus' presence and the enlargement of any healthy feeling.

Please remember this is not a judgement time, as it is an encounter time with God and with yourself.

Noticing is the primary goal, and you are able to do that only if you are in the present moment, so throughout this exercise of mindfulness keep your mind in the present moment, and use the breathing as leverage to help you to do it.

Chapter Thirteen
Sowing the Future

As we have seen, we sow the future today, and Galatians 6:7 tells us we will reap what we sow. But I want to consider an interesting point; I once read a quote that said, in effect, 'We can't choose what we reap, but we can choose what we sow.'[55]

This could really give me peace about my future, because if I can't choose what I reap, then I don't have to worry about it.

But I believe this quote raises two questions, and I think it it is worth exploring them.

The first question

The first has to do with how often we seem to reap results that, in spite of being planted with love, are affected by life's anomalies – how often do the storms of life, morning frosts or droughts ravage what we have planted? How many times do bosses destroy our confidence, friends abandon us, or families betray us, and therefore bring a harvest of difficult things into our lives?

---

[55] Source unknown.

Between the time of planting and the harvest, between the dream and its realisation, many things are going to happen in our lives that shoot us down or discourage us over which we have no control, whether they come through other people, the economy or religion. These are the weather conditions of life, which cannot be avoided or even prepared for in advance. In nature, we cannot control whether it rains too much or doesn't rain at all – both equally damaging to the crop.

We have already learned how God turns our tragedies into passions and our failures into blessings, and how we have to take control of our lives, so as to live them with greater wisdom and pleasure. But in life we will have to deal with circumstances that we would rather not encounter, which are also part of our journey; the curses that God turns into blessings.

All of us will have problems, whether we sow or not, so I believe that it is better to sow. What I sow is really more important than the storms I will encounter. I believe the rain will fall just as much on the land that has been cultivated as on the land that has not, but after one season one of them will be full of worthless things, while the other, in spite of the problems, will be full of flowers and good fruits.

In short, we may go through many trials during our lives, and at times we may wonder if we really are reaping what we have sown. But it is still important to keep sowing, every day, trusting God to work out the ultimate end result. We have to remember that we do not have the whole picture. I may sow good and not always seem to reap it. But for the Christian, we can be content in knowing that God is in control, and we must keep sowing positively.

In regard to sowing into the future financially: I have many friends and counselling clients who are desperate to acquire more than just a nest egg in order to have a secure future. Of course, I am not denying that some people will be rich, but a happy person is wealthier than a rich person who is sad.

The real question is what we have set our hearts on, who or what is our main treasure in life. Nothing can take the place of God in our lives: neither money, nor marriage, nor children, nor beauty. Even though I believe there are many things that can make us happy, like our children, our studies, our football team or new clothes, I do believe that the greatest happiness of all is found in God, who is the author of today. In Luke 12, Jesus warns us to avoid all forms of greed, because 'life does not consist in an abundance of possessions' (verse 15).

I am not criticising people who have money, just those who set their hearts on money instead of on God, who is the provider of everything we have.

It is more important to know how much things are worth than how much they cost. It is more important to be happy in what we are doing today than to have money, because nothing is of higher value than that.

The second question

Coming back to the quote: 'We can't choose what we reap, but we can choose what we sow', the second question to be addressed is: why should I worry about the future, since it hasn't happened yet and won't even happen if I don't sow now in my present? Once again, I challenge you to live today to the fullest, because the future will only happen because the now exists, and it is in the now that we decide what it will be like. My future depends on my present. The present is where we sow and water our future, so our future is entirely dependent upon it.

We can't stop working because we say that the future doesn't belong to us – only the present – because that would be a mistake. What we need to learn is that the fact that we aren't sure what is going to happen tomorrow should give us peace. The book of Proverbs 27:1 says, 'Do not boast about tomorrow, for you do not know what a day may bring.' It does no good to boast ahead of time because tomorrow depends on the Lord.

I bought an apartment in 2007 and, at that time, the economy had not stopped growing. In the previous ten years, the price of houses had doubled where I live, and I was doing what everyone else was doing – buying a home. Because I'm always reading about the economy, I knew that a crisis would come, but I never imagined that it would be so big. I can testify that, as the Word of God says, we don't know what tomorrow will bring. What could be a reason for pride can also be a reason for concern, but both before and after buying my home, my goal has been to live for each day.

When we live for today, we have to keep our dreams in mind; we have to think about whether what we are planting today will help us to fulfil them. What we can't do is wait until our dreams are fulfilled to be happy; we have to be happy in the process.

A woodworking friend of mine once told me that he loves to see a piece finished and installed, but what he loves the most is cutting and shaping the wood. He said that he feels like a doctor in the operating room doing plastic surgery on the wood, so it will look like what he wants it to.

In addition to what the Word says about no one being sure about the future, it also says in Ecclesiastes 11:2 that, since we don't know what is going to happen tomorrow, and given the possibility that something unexpected will happen, a good way to avoid failure is to diversify our investments. Many people, anxious to profit in the easiest way possible, invest everything in one place. This thirst for a prosperous future is the result of what happens when we don't know how to live today or walk in the wisdom of the Word of God.

When I think about tomorrow, I remind myself that the only sure thing in life is death, and the only thing that I will take with me is the time that I spent here doing what God wanted me to do and fulfilling my destiny. Through my time of study and my attendance at various funerals, I have learned that this is the only thing I will take with me from here. After all, I have never seen a removal van at a funeral. I have heard that the Egyptian pharaohs tried to do that, but centuries later we can see that they never used anything they tried to take with them, and what was not stolen from them is now in museums. Our goal is to plant today in order to reap in the future, but today we need to harvest what we planted in the past. It does no good to leave it in the garden, because it will dry up, and it does no good to build silos to keep it in.

We often make plans for the future, but we don't even know for sure what will happen five minutes from now, because it doesn't belong to us alone, but to God. We need to do our part – work, get ready – but we can't count our chickens before they are hatched.

God has grand plans for us as well, but He doesn't want us to sacrifice our daily happiness for some future happiness, because if we live only for the future, today will have no value, and if the future doesn't turn out the way we hoped, we will have lost both the present and the future.

If we live only for the future and don't take advantage of today, we will be anxious about everything, as Jesus says in Matthew 6. What I recommend is not that we stop dreaming or struggling and certainly not that we stop sowing; it is as we do all those things that we make the most of every moment, trusting that the God who controls all things wants the best for us. He, who is a much better Father than our earthly father, will keep His promise to take care of us. We need to be confident that He will supply all things and give us much more than we ask or think.[56] The God who kept His promises to the people of Israel will also do the same in our lives now, so that we can live today in the confidence of a better tomorrow.

Reflection Time

The quote we have looked at says we don't always reap what we sow. But, as Christians, we know that ultimately

---

[56] See Ephesians 3:20.

we will reap a harvest, because this is what the Word of God teaches.[57] There may be troubles on the way, but we need to keep sowing. We must trust God with our future and depend on Him, not on wealth or material things, for security.

- How would you like to be remembered? No one will talk about your cash; they may talk a little bit about your accomplishments and work achievements, but mainly they will talk about the difference you made in their lives and the legacy you left.

- Based on that, how would you like to be remembered by:

  o Family?

  o Friends?

  o Colleagues?

- What can you begin to do today so that the memory of your life reaps a good harvest?

---

[57] See Galatians 6:9.

Chapter Fourteen
Postponing Joy

I realise that we have been discussing the future and its uncertainties, including the financial aspects of the future. I believe that financial stability is pertinent to all of us and is often a cause of stress in our lives if it is not well handled. To show how important this topic is in our daily lives, Jesus mentions finances in sixteen of His thirty-eight parables;[58] so nearly half of them dealt with this subject.

However, what concerns me more than financial security is our tendency to postpone our happiness until the future and forget to live today. Yes, we need to plant today to have a respectable and prosperous future, but we can't wait until that happens for us to be happy, for in the end, 'This is the day that the LORD has made; let us rejoice and be glad in it.'[59]

Many people, however, do hope that things will turn out in a way that makes them happy. For example, it's widespread among young people to hope for happiness after they get married. I know this from personal experience. Single people hope that the other person will

[58] https://www.preachingtoday.com/illustrations/1996/decembe r/410.html (accessed 24th October 2018).
[59] Psalm 118:24, NRSV.

make them complete so that then they can enjoy life. The truth is, though, that we are complete in ourselves, and our happiness depends on us and not on another person. If we are happy when we are single, we will be happy when we are married; if we are unhappy when we are single, we will be when we are married too.

Another thing that single people do is postpone until marriage things they could do alone or with friends, such as travelling or buying a house. They don't do things that would make them happy, and instead put all their hope in the future – an uncertain future that may or may not happen – because they don't know if they will get married or not, nor do they know if their other half will be 'perfect' or not!

Besides single people, obsessive workers wait until they retire to fulfil their dreams, in the hope that in the future they will be able to take all the trips they never took, or catch all the fish they never caught, or make all the clothes they never made.

As we have seen, we don't know when the future will arrive, so we have to do a little of everything today. It does no good for me to want to start my diet on Monday, because Monday will never come; what *will* occur is the moment in which I decide to start and from then on change my behaviour. I'm sure you've promised yourself many times that you would start your diet on Monday or have started exercising on New Year's Day. Maybe you even joined a gym and paid for several months, but you never went. I know, because I've done the same thing.

Our future is planted today, so we need to be more concerned about today than about the future. Today I need to have the right attitude about what I want in life. If I do, I can set priorities that will help me reach my life's goal and help me fulfil my mission.

If I want to be healthy in the future, I shouldn't wait until I get there to take care of myself; I should know and follow instructions on how to be healthy every day. As for our family, we can't wait until our children are teenagers to spend time with them or wait until we have money to go out with them. We need to work on the way we relate with family members and friends every day. We need to make new friends every day, and the friendships we already have need to be maintained. We have opportunities to develop friendships every day, whether at work, at church, in the neighbourhood or with relatives.

Every day we build our future, so we need to make every day count. We need to work hard to make our day a pleasant one and sow for a better future. Every day we need to practise having good thoughts, which enable us to reach goals and so attain a rich and full life.

If we do these things, we will sow powerful thoughts every day and develop ideas for our future. What we think produces strength in us to carry on and also generates the words our mouth will speak, because it is out of what fills our hearts that we speak.[60]

Our thoughts, however, must be accompanied by faith, because it is faith that touches the heart of God and moves the mountains in our lives. Along with our thinking, we need to live out our faith and deepen it with Bible reading and ongoing dialogue with God.

---

[60] See Luke 6:45.

Personal growth results from practising these small but very important daily habits. We will see personal development take place in the spiritual area of our lives, in an increase in our faith, and the resulting increase in our ability to reflect Christ to the world as if we were a perfect mirror, as well as in our relationships with our family and friends.

For our lives to be a masterpiece, however, it isn't enough to only think about it or work towards it. We need to do both. John Maxwell[61] summarised how to create a rich and full life as follows:

How to Create a Masterpiece

Good choices minus Daily discipline = Plans without results
Daily discipline minus Good choices = Rigidness without rewards
Good choices plus Daily Discipline = A masterpiece in progress

Choose well today and have a better tomorrow, for your future begins today.

When making a decision:
Don't do it because it's EASY.
Don't do it because it's INEXPENSIVE.
Don't do it because it's POPULAR.
Do it because it's RIGHT.

---

[61] John Maxwell, *Faça o hoje valer a pena* (Make Today Count) (Nashville, TN: FaithWords, 2008), p11.

Reflection Time

- Based on John Maxwell's path to creating a masterpiece, could you list the following:

  o Good choices that you must make.

  o Daily disciplines that you have to follow (remember that to change a habit you need twenty-one days, but to grow a new pathway you need sixty-three days doing the same new habit).

Chapter Fifteen

The Value of the Day of Small Beginnings

Mariana got up early and went to the gym. She wanted to lose a few pounds, but mostly she just wanted to get in shape.

Since it was her first day, she took a class on how to use the equipment and spent some time talking with a personal trainer. He told Mariana that it wouldn't be possible to reach all of her goals in a week, and maybe not even in a few months, because it would take time to get in shape. He told her that there would be good days, when weight loss and muscle-building would happen quickly, and other days when she would feel like she wasn't getting anywhere. There would be days when she would move on to more difficult exercises and days when she would maintain what she had already achieved. This would happen because the exercises were designed to push the muscle to its limits and then relax it.

This principle from physical workouts applies to the rest of our lives as well and is vital to our growth. We go through challenging things that seem to be bigger than we are, and when we look back at them, we see that we have been stretched to our limits. When we are running on the treadmill and get close to our limits, it feels like there is a wall in our way, and our minds seem to tell us that there is no way we can keep on running or walking; even if our muscles can handle it, our mind refuses. At that moment, when we look at that wall, there is only one person who can conquer it and tear it down – and that is we ourselves.

Some marathon runners train physically, to build up their muscles and endurance, but they also train mentally, with the help of trainers and psychologists, to overcome that barrier to finishing the race. Then, when their brain tells them that there is no hope, that the body can't do it, they will have learned to be their own masters and will say to themselves that it can, and go on to finish the race.

Remember, you can overcome that obstacle; you can win that mental battle. Our minds are always telling us that we can do some things and not others, but it's up to us to determine what we can or cannot do.

Every time we get close to reaching our limit, we are tested and ask ourselves if it is worth it to keep fighting the battle. For Mariana, her first few days of exercising were the worst, for it made her very sore, and she wanted to quit.

Everything we do in life has its day of small beginnings. Before we start to walk, we crawl, then we begin to stand up holding on to something, followed by standing unassisted and taking our first steps, until we master the technique of walking across the room. Before long we begin to run and jump, but it all started with that very first day.

Even though we know this, we can make the mistake of sabotaging our dreams of the future as well as our present, just because we don't know how to make the most of our days of small beginnings.

We want our fields to be ready to harvest even before we've done the hard work of planting, fertilising and watering. I'm going through days of small beginnings in many areas of my life right now, and I have to ask myself if I'm going to keep going in all of them, or only in some of them. I do know, though, that if I don't stay committed to the ones I believe in and dream about, I won't get anywhere. The days of small beginnings are slow and arduous; they are hard and make our muscles sore, and we are only going to keep going if we have hope that everything will eventually get better and it will have been worth the trouble. However, joy doesn't have to be postponed until that happens; it is available now, today, in the celebration of today and in knowing that these are the days that will make our dreams come true.

It is the same way in our spiritual lives. The Word of God tells us that we are all running to attain an 'imperishable crown',[62] but that to run this race we have to train by doing spiritual exercises, spend plenty of time stretching with our knees to the ground in prayer, and jump many obstacles, in faith that it will bring us victory. As we follow this spiritual training programme, we will continuously reflect Christ's glory more and more in our lives.

Great athletes are known for their moments of glory in the Olympics; their names are recorded when they score the winning goal in championships; but in every case, they

---

[62] 1 Corinthians 9:25, NKJV.

started out one day very humbly. Some of them were even told that they had no talent, but they didn't despise their days of small beginnings; on the contrary, they held on to their determination to attain victory. And when that day of victory finally arrives, they celebrate it, realising that this day has been constructed slowly over a long period of time – years or even decades of giving their best efforts every day to their training, and sowing hard work and joy in the now of many past moments. They did so, believing that when the future arrived, the victories they won day after day would be evidenced in a great victory and a great present.

This reminds me of Hillsong Church in Australia, which started out with forty-five members and today has churches in many countries, as well as CDs and books that are known worldwide, programmes on television and the internet, podcasts, and many other ministries. Their story encourages us not to 'despise the day of small things [beginnings]', as Zechariah 4:10 tells us. I am also reminded of the classic example of Abraham Lincoln, who lost many elections before being elected president of the United States, and ending up being acclaimed as one of its greatest presidents.

We have to fight to make our dreams come true, whether we have a lot of education or very little. Whether we are in school or not, whether we come from a wealthy family or not, whether we are rich or poor, we need to learn not to despise a single day in our lives. Every day is special and will take us to better days, in which we can attain still more victories.

Paul said in Philippians 4:11-13 how he learned to live fully every day of his life:

> I am not saying this because I am in need, for I have learned to be content whatever the circumstances. I know what it is to be in need, and I know what it is to have plenty. I have learned the secret of being content in any and every situation, whether well fed or hungry, whether living in plenty or in want. I can do all this through him who gives me strength.

Every day is very important. We construct our tomorrow every day. We need to value today in order to triumph over today and, as a result, achieve a better future. After all, the day of small beginnings is as precious as the day of victory, for one cannot take place without the other.

Never think that the day you are living in is just another day. Never despise it, because something can happen in what seems to be an ordinary day that will change your life forever.

Let us always be ready to be conquerors; let us value every day, beginning with the day of small beginnings.

Reflection Time

In Matthew 17:20, Jesus is recorded as saying: 'Truly I tell you, if you have faith as small as a mustard seed, you can say to this mountain, "Move from here to there," and it will move. Nothing will be impossible for you.'

Therefore, on the days of small beginnings, we need a little faith to move forward, knowing that He is able to help us.

- Based on that, and thinking about your current circumstances, what do you have 'a little faith' for today?

Chapter Sixteen

Turning the Day of Trouble into a Day of Joy

It was already two o'clock in the afternoon, and Joana was still seated at the kitchen table. She had finished lunch some time ago but didn't have the energy to get up. Her life was really hard, and it seemed like her pain-filled days would never end.

It had been more than two months since she had lost her job, and everything about her life was difficult. Her savings had run out, and she didn't know what to do, as her children were in school and she had no way to pay the school fees. In addition, her water and electricity bills were overdue.

Joana was going through a time of great stress, as many are today. At times like these, we have a tendency to give in to habits that are bad for our health, like smoking, drinking or overeating. These are some of the outlets we look towards to alleviate our stress.

In actuality, however, these things are just a means of 'escape', to get our attention off our problems and feel some relief, to forget for a moment that we are going through a difficult time. Over time, these escape routes end up impacting our health in various ways, from extreme weight loss or weight gain to chemical dependency. They don't help solve anything; they just create a bigger problem that covers up the original one.

How many alcoholics use drink to cover up the emotional effects of a ruined marriage, how many teenagers use drugs because their parents don't pay attention to them, and how many people work harder and harder to cover up with their computer the fact that they have a hard time relating to other people?

In times of suffering, what can we do, what can we believe in? Maybe we can't even think about tomorrow; after all, it doesn't even seem like today exists. Our strength is gone, and when we say anything, it is to accuse God. We complain, loudly and clearly, that He is silent when we need Him the most. We interpret His silence to mean that the God of the impossible has decided to do even less than what is possible and has refused to intervene in our lives.

In Psalm 50:1 the psalmist says that it is God who brings forth a new day in our lives; it is He who makes the world turn, calling forth a new day so that His children can enjoy His presence one more time, and have one more day for the praise of the glory of His grace, as Paul tells us in Ephesians 1. We know that struggles and suffering do come, bringing fear along with them, but God tells us in Psalm 50:15: 'Call on me in the day of trouble; I will deliver you, and you will honour me.' Once again, I see that it is not our job to struggle with the world or even with Satan;[63]

---

[63] Although we are called to 'Resist him' – see 1 Peter 5:9.

that is God's job. He will deliver us; we need only give Him all the credit and honour for the victory.

At times like this, I remind myself of the testimonies of all the men and women of God who describe how they had nothing to eat but trusted in God in their day of trouble, and He came to them and provided for them, not only that day but also in the following days. Our God teaches us to live in dependence on Him every day and seek Him for the strength to live one day at a time. The most important thing is to trust in God.

Another thing we need to learn is to have faith in ourselves to make it through difficult and painful times, because often we have faith in God, but we don't have faith that He will use us. God calls us to do great things with our lives, but sometimes along the way we lose our faith in our own calling and we begin to sink, just as Peter did when he walked on water.[64] He knew, however, that Jesus could help him in that situation so he called out to Him, and He answered.

In the day of trouble, we get lost, and we don't believe that God can use us. But I want to remind you that our God is the One who turns our tears to joy, so we can take the medicine prescribed in Proverbs 17:22: 'A cheerful heart is good medicine, but a crushed spirit dries up the bones.'

Remember, every day is special. To give you an example, I want to tell you a story that taught me to see

---

64 See Matthew 14:22-33.

that a day can be transformed and can transform the rest of our lives.[65]

A woman was standing in an airport in the United States, and she was crying. A man stopped and asked her what she was crying about. She answered that it was because her father had died. They talked for a little while, and the man missed his flight. The man told her that he would be shooting a movie in her city and asked her to come and see him to tell him how she was doing.

A few months later, she was driving along when she saw a traffic jam up ahead and realised the delay was being caused by a movie that was being made. She remembered then that the man who had helped her in the airport had said he would be there making a movie. Even so, she didn't think any more about it and continued on her way. On the way back, however, she decided to stop and go to the area. She decided to tell her story to a security guard. And again, she met the man who was her good Samaritan – Kevin Costner.

As if the whole situation wasn't already exciting enough, because certainly all of us would like to have such a famous good Samaritan help us out, Costner invited her to stay and watch the filming. Then a man who was producing the movie began to explain to her what was happening. They became friends, and a while later they got married!

Never despise a single day, even if it starts out terribly, because you never know how God might transform it. We

[65] http://joelosteen-itsyourtime.blogspot.com/2009/11/its-your-time-all-things-work-together.html (accessed 31st October 2018). Paraphrased.

need to make sure that He is always the ruler of our day. Of course, I know that 'Jesus wept'[66] and also that He went through terrible suffering before His death, so I know that there will be days in which we also are going to cry, but we can never give up; we can never live without hope that things will get better, because even in His death Jesus brought us life.

Let's look at the case of Jesus. The night before His death He was in Gethsemane sweating blood and asking God that, if possible, that cup could be taken from Him.[67] However, God's will was done, and He suffered there on the cross for all of us. It was a day of trouble for Him and for all of His followers. It seemed like everything Jesus had taught – along with this new movement – had died, since its leader had also died.

The disciples returned to their old professions. The women wept. It seemed like everything that had happened was history now and would live on only in their minds. However, that day of trouble turned into a day of blessing on Sunday. The day of trouble was just the day that needed to happen before the great victory. And I believe that the same thing is true in our lives.

If every day is special, can one day be worth more than another? The Bible says that it can, and that day, interestingly enough, can happen every day, for what the Word tells us is that one day in the Lord's presence is worth more 'than a thousand elsewhere' (Psalm 84:10). So, we need to believe in our days, in fact in all of them, and get rid of the idea once and for all that when we get such-and-

---

[66] John 11:35.
[67] See Luke 22:39-44.

such an opportunity, or when we become so-and-so, we will be able to do this or that. We are masters of our destiny, and we have to write it every day. When you arrive in heaven, you won't be able to justify yourself before God by saying that you had wanted to be a better employee, but your boss didn't let you, or you had wanted to be a better husband, but you married the wrong woman.

You may have a day when everything is difficult at work, and you wonder why there are so many problems. Imagine what it would be like if there were no problems at work. A job without problems would be easy, and if it were easy, it could be done by someone less qualified than you who makes half of what you make. So, we could say that half of your salary comes from solving problems and dealing with difficult situations.

So then, praise God for that problem, and for that job you have, because there are a lot of people who don't have a job or who earn half of what you do just because they don't have the same problems. Always believe that God has something better for you, but be happy today.

Some of the times of trouble in our lives, or decisions that seem to be wrong, or pursuits that seem to go nowhere – days that seem to be wasted – in fact may be days in which God is very much in control, in which He wants to take us somewhere for some reason, as He did with Israel's first king, Saul. Before Saul was anointed king of Israel, he was sent out to look for his father's donkeys and spent several days searching for them until he got so fed up that he decided to go back home, thinking that by then his family would have become more worried about him and his servant than the donkeys. However, his servant

128

suggested that they should go to see a man of God who was in a nearby town.

When they arrived there, the prophet Samuel saw that the young man who was approaching was the man God had chosen to be the new king of Israel, and he said, 'I am the seer … Go up ahead of me to the high place, for today you are to eat with me, and in the morning I will send you on your way and will tell you all that is in your heart. As for the donkeys you lost three days ago, do not worry about them; they have been found' (1 Samuel 9:19-20). During that meeting, Samuel anointed Saul king of Israel.

Once again God used his own methods to bring blessing. Many times, what seems to be a series of conflicts and mishaps is, in fact, the means God is using to put us in certain places for a period of time, for us to be blessed and for us to be a blessing.

Joana's story also had a happy ending, and she came to see that the clouds that were surrounding her and closing in were in fact there to pour out showers of blessing. She got a new job, in which she had a much better relationship with her boss, in an area of work that she liked much more because it involved helping older people. It fulfilled two of her life goals: both a higher salary and a higher social purpose.

Reflection Time

In Acts 16, we read how Paul and Silas were in an inner cell of a prison, with their feet securely fastened. Then in verses 25 and 26 we read:

About midnight *Paul and Silas were praying and singing hymns to God*, and the other prisoners were listening to them. Suddenly there was such a violent earthquake that the foundations of the prison were shaken. At once all the prison doors flew open, and everyone's chains came loose. (my emphasis)

I believe there is a fantastic power when we say to God, 'Thank You for what has happened in my life, I praise You for what you have done, and I worship You for who You are.'

The worship has impressive power because when we worship, we are just thanking God for being who He is; we are honouring Him for who He is. I believe we are just fulfilling our purpose according to Ephesians 1:6 as we are created 'to the praise of his glorious grace'.

Let's do that, then!

- Thank God for something that has happened or for a relationship you have.

- Praise God for something He has done.

- Worship God for who He is.

Chapter Seventeen

Defeating the Giants in Your Day

It's six o'clock in the morning and the alarm clock goes off. Paulo cannot believe that the night has gone by so quickly and thinks, 'Can it really be time to get up already?' He looks at the clock radio, hits the snooze button and goes back to sleep, knowing that nine minutes later it will ring again, and feeling he needs that extra time.

The alarm goes off again. Paulo sits up in bed and thinks, 'It was a good night, short as it was, but now my nightmares begin all over again.' And so it goes every day of his life. His refuge is his night's sleep, which only comes with the help of medication, a time when he apparently switches off his problems, but they return with the daylight. It seems like everything is going wrong, and it's no coincidence that he has real persecutors who put him down all day long.

Every morning Paulo speaks positive words to himself to try to keep his spirits up, but it doesn't change the fact that he undergoes persecution the rest of the day. His boss never leaves him alone; he gives him extra work all the time; he changes the schedule and doesn't tell him. Paulo doesn't even take a lunch break any more and works late every night, but still his boss has never noticed. He is giving his all, but he never receives a word of commendation. On the contrary, he is criticised all the time and feels like he is walking a tightrope. He continually thinks he will be the next person to be fired and has not enjoyed his work for a long time. Now all he feels is fear, pain and discouragement, but he continues to work there because he thinks there is no other solution.

Paulo spends the whole day in fear and anxiety, worrying about his job, but he doesn't quit, because he believes that if he loses it, he won't be able to pay the rent on his house, keep up his car payments, buy groceries or realise his dream of marrying his girlfriend.

The Bible tells us that David experienced a similar situation. In Psalm 56 he talks about the fear he had of losing his life, for his persecutors attacked him every day, and he felt like they did so all day long. This kind of attack is the worst, for it is very difficult for us to stay alert at every moment, because that would require constant vigilance and we just don't have the strength to keep that up for long periods of time.

Paulo was experiencing this every day, and at the weekends, when he didn't go to work and could spend time with his friends, family and girlfriend, he would continue to be tormented by his thoughts. Whenever he looked at his girlfriend, he would think about how he would never realise his dream of marrying her; whenever he listened to his friends talking about their jobs and how successful they were, he would get upset and walk away; if anyone complained about work, he had a worse story to tell them. All because of the pressure and the constant war being waged in his mind.

He was losing the battle; it dominated his thinking. Even when he tried to change his situation at work, it seemed like everyone used his words against him. 'All day long they twist my words; all their schemes are for my ruin' (Psalm 56:5). The truth is that because we live in an imperfect world, we are always persecuted. There are times when we feel more oppressed than others, but the truth is that there will always be those who are against us.

I believe that there is a remedy for this world, and that is Jesus Christ and the love that He pours out in all who live in Him, which enables us to accept one another's differences. We are all unique in this world, but for things to go right, we must take that medicine. We need to understand that the world changes when we change, and our day changes when we change how we approach it.

A great man once put a sign on his mirror that said, 'You are face to face with the person who is responsible for your happiness today.' He realised that everything that would happen in his day would be directly affected by how he looked at it, and on the value he would place on it. And we should realise the same thing.

We need to decide to guard our minds. We need to determine what we think about, day and night, for we can either live in the problem or in hope; we can either live believing in a God who is small and cannot help us, or in a God who is always bigger than our problems and can come to our aid.

I am reminded of David going out to face Goliath. His focus could have been on the size of the giant, which was real and right in front of him, but he preferred to speak out the name of God; he preferred to focus on his God and not on the problem. Throughout most of the passage in 1 Samuel 17, David talks about God, and the power He has to resolve any situation; he speaks very little about his problem.

We can also see that when Jesus was being interrogated before His crucifixion, His focus was on God and doing His Father's will. Just like David, Jesus refused to look at the problem; He looked at the God who could transform the situation.

The Word tells us that when we face problems, we should cry out to God, for He listens to our prayers. We can't let ourselves be paralysed, like the people of Israel before Goliath and the Philistines. They spent forty days doing nothing, overcome with anxiety and fear. We have to be brave and take hold of the Word of God unless the Lord leads us to stay in prayer. My wife and I prayed for forty days about a decision we had to make. From the first day on, we expected an answer, but it didn't come until the thirty-ninth day. God was faithful and always will be.

We should not be afraid to take the initiative, for God is with us. As our Father, He has something special planned for us, and He calls us to draw near to Him, and so invites us to live an abundant life full of His Spirit in our daily lives.

We know this, but because we doubt, because we feel like we are alone, we let the battle in our minds be lost. Because we waver, because we become fearful and pay attention only to what we see and the pressure we feel all around us, we think that the enemy is stronger. At this point in the battle, we are already tired, and that affects our hearts. We shake with fatigue, and our body begins to give up. Fatigue is not just at the door; it has already come in and is sitting in the living room drinking a soft drink and watching television. It is already in charge and is calling its partner, depression, to come to visit us because there is an empty bedroom to stay in.

So, is it all over? There's nowhere left to run or any hope; so, what should we do now? Or what should we stop doing? If there is no hope, why keep on fighting? Why try to do anything different? Why would Paulo try to change his boss or try to be noticed some other way? The only decision left to him is to live in bitterness for the rest of his life and accept that it has to be that way – that's just the way life is – or to throw everything up in the air and leave with no idea where he is going.

Some people even think that life isn't worth living, like those who think life is over after the stock market crashes and kill themselves, or those who, out of despair, think about cutting a part of their bodies to get stability and relieve the pressure they feel inside, while others find consolation in food.

I once watched a documentary[68] on tattooing, and the reporter was looking through a book of designs when he came across the word 'loser'. Curious, he asked the tattoo artist if anyone dared to get a tattoo of a word like that. When he answered affirmatively, he asked him what type of person would do that, and the artist told him that it was people who had lost all hope.

---

[68] Documentary unknown.

What to do at that point? Call out to God to come and rescue us? Could crying out to Him for help be the solution? The writer of Psalm 102 cries out to God to hear his prayer, but it actually seems like he doesn't believe that God will hear him. In the anguish of his soul, he sees his days dissipating like smoke. He feels like his days are being shortened, that his life is cut short and that soon it will be over. Like this person, our friend Paulo is probably asking himself: 'Why make my girlfriend wait forever? Why don't we live together without getting married, or why don't I rob someone or do something else illegal to get myself out of this situation? If there is no hope, then why try to do things right?'

David had opportunities to take that route. His problems could have been solved quickly and easily just by killing King Saul, which would be against the law but would resolve the situation. If that happened, he would no longer be persecuted and would even take his enemy's place as king. He had two opportunities to kill the king, to take vengeance, but he decided to stand firm in his convictions and wait for the right time for things to happen, since God is in control of everything.

And what about us, who live in a world where everything happens instantaneously, where the internet connects us to the other side of the planet? Are we prepared to wait for the right time? God presents us with difficult situations so that we can be tested, so that we can get the proper perspective on our lives and on who we are because of Him. In those situations, He is the One who can act, not us; it is He who can do something, not us. It is His intention to show us that only He is worthy of all honour, glory, praise and exaltation.

When I say this, I'm talking about our hearts and minds being full of Him, for many times we want a miracle, a change in our situation, and victory, but when it comes, we give all the credit to our own abilities, and maybe to the contacts and friends we made along the way, and we forget what He has done. We also sometimes celebrate what He has done only in terms of the fact that it was done and not for who He is.

So then, tests are an opportunity for us to draw close to God, to put our focus in the right place and so praise Him, give Him all the credit and exalt Him as Lord of our lives.

Psalm 102 promises us victory when we put our lives in proper perspective before the throne of God. Actually, it only promises us victory if we follow the path that our exalted God shows us, the one by which we recognise who He is for us.

For David, he did get the victory; all his dreams were realised and his destiny was fulfilled, all in due time. So, what he needed to do every day was not worry about tomorrow or make millions of plans to make sure that everything would work out right or constantly relive yesterday's persecutions. He didn't need to plan his future or relive his past; he simply prayed and put everything in God's hands, and so had time to live in the present.

Paulo lost his job and was without hope for a period, for he had fought to keep his job and had suffered a lot of humiliation because he felt secure only when he was at work. He went through some difficult days, but reflecting on James 4:14, which says that our life is like a 'mist that appears for a little while and then vanishes', he came to realise that everything is temporary, and it is impossible to be certain of tomorrow.

Upon reflection, he also realised that God was telling him that instead of depending on himself, he should trust in the Creator of history, who turns the hearts of kings, controls the fate of peoples and uses the enemy of our souls himself for our good.

There is something we usually don't mention when we think of things that build a person's character or build someone's future, but I believe it is an instrument God uses. That is the rejections that we receive. These rejections are good because, first of all, they are doors that God has closed for us, so they are therefore not in His plans for our lives, and secondly, they help to build our character, just as they help to stretch us beyond our current capacities.

The rejection of a girlfriend or boyfriend can be the means to better interactions with the next, just like a 'no' in an interview can be a lesson that helps us succeed in the next one, or a refused visa can open the door to another country or provide confirmation that God does not want us in a certain place. We need to trust that He guides us by the 'yes' and the 'no' we experience, as well as the times of waiting.

What we need to learn is that the God of David is our God as well.

In time God opened the door to another job for Paulo, fulfilling a dream that he had given up hope of ever coming true.

Reflection Time

The people of Israel were stuck for forty days, looking to the giant and afraid of taking action, when David appeared and confronted Goliath in the name of the Lord, the God of Israel.

To defeat the giant, we need to go to war. The worst thing when confronted by a giant is that we become paralysed; we do not run, we do not confront, we lose time, and the enemy freezes us.

- What in your life is paralysing you? What in your life is confronting you, and you are taking no action?

- It is time now to look these things in the eye and say that you are able to defeat them because you have a God who is by your side?

- List the things that you have to take action on.

- Now pray over them.

- Now write the actions you need to take to defeat them.

Chapter Eighteen

Learning About Today in the School of Life

'This is the day that the LORD has made; let us rejoice and be glad in it'[69] – for, after all, we have many things to celebrate. Today will be filled with pleasure because we are going to go through it at God's side and we will be 'more than conquerors'.[70]

We should have this confidence every day of our lives, but maybe you aren't so sure; perhaps your problems and daily pressures have derailed you, as they can for all of us.

I really don't know the secret to life, but I believe that one of the greatest tips we can follow is to look at everything from a positive point of view. Right now, I have a job that is relatively easy to handle, without a great deal of internal pressure, but when I come home, I spend the first hour listening to my wife telling me about all the pressures that she has felt. I think a lot about this and I have put the situation before God, asking Him to find another job for her. In fact I get so troubled that sometimes I end up

---

[69] Psalm 118:24, NRSV.
[70] Romans 8:37.

getting confused and saying things I shouldn't, but one thing I can say: that pressure has helped her to grow a lot, to learn to be a leader, to organise her time, to dress better and to study harder, so I can say that because of it she has grown as a person in a substantial way. So, is pressure really something terrible for us, or can it be good in some ways?

An excellent example of how it can be a positive thing is school exams. If they didn't exist, we would probably go through school without learning anything, without having reached our goal, because it is the pressure of grades that makes us study and grow as a result.

Even extreme pressure that crushes us does us good. Let me make it very clear that I am not a masochist, but life has taught me that we have a lot to learn, even through rejection, and for me, there is probably no greater pressure than that.

I believe that we are formed in life by the 'yes', 'no' and 'wait' that we receive every day. What we are today is the result of these seeds that were planted. For some, a 'no' means an ending, while to others it means that they should try again in another way. But even more important than the 'yes' or the 'no' is the realisation that our God is in control of everything and that 'all things work together for [our] good'.[71]

Today we think, mainly because of modern theology, that God has to keep all of His promises, and we have to live a life of prosperity. I agree with this, for our God is faithful to do everything He promises, but I am not sure

---

[71] Romans 8:28, NKJV.

that this means a life of financial wealth and promises of financial success.

I believe that God always has the best planned for us and I also believe that this 'best' gets better every day to the degree that we develop our relationship with Him through worship and obedience. As we develop our relationship with God, we go through things that prepare us for a better future, full of His presence. Along the way, we experience the pressures that come from situations of rejection, from financial stress or from the natural stresses of life, like work, the death of a loved one, or family problems.

If we look at the life of Moses, we see that first of all, as a baby, he was found and adopted by Pharaoh's daughter. Later he was rejected by the Egyptians and by the Israelites when he killed a man, so he went to live in the desert, where he was accepted by the family of Jethro and married one of his daughters. Forty years later, God appears to Moses and chooses him to free the people of Israel. God chooses him and accepts him as he is, but Moses is afraid that the people will reject him again and tries to talk God out of His choice, but God commands him to go.[72] From there he goes on to become the greatest leader in Jewish history until the coming of the Messiah, Jesus Christ.

Moses was shaped by the acceptance and rejection that he received from people throughout his life. We can see how God was controlling his story the whole time: first arranging for him to study in the best schools in Egypt and then having him take a practical survival course in the

---

[72] You can read this part of his story in Exodus 2-4.

desert so that he would be able to guide the people for forty years.

Another great man who learned to live with acceptance and rejection was the one responsible for taking the people to Egypt in the first place. He was a dear son who experienced highs and lows, going from favourite son to slave to manager, and from manager to prisoner to second-in-command in Pharaoh's kingdom. That man is Joseph, whom we thought about earlier in this book. When we look at Joseph's story, it reads like a movie or a fairy tale in which the street urchin becomes a prince or the beggar becomes king, but in real life it was a great battle won through the apprenticeship of times of acceptance and rejection. Even though he fought many battles – the rejection and betrayal by his brothers, his life as a slave in Egypt, an unjust accusation, prison – he continued to trust that God was in control of the situation. And when he was reunited with his brothers, he did not seek revenge. He understood that they were only part of the plan that God had for his life, that the rejection was used by God to bring direction to his life and forge his character.

I believe that this is why God tells us that we are to rejoice every day. After all, He owns all our days and is in control of all things, whether good or seemingly bad, and He will use all of them to move us towards our destiny – if we allow Him to.

We need to learn how to depend on Him in all things, but for this to happen we have to renew our thinking. We need to learn, first of all, that God is in control of everything and, secondly, that situations that seem to be bad because they put pressure on us can bring with them fresh starts and new opportunities.

In order to realise their destiny, some people have to go through a time of loss and others through a period of financial hardship, just as Moses had to face the desert for some years in order to realise that God's plan to free the people were different from his. Joseph, even though he had a dream in which his brothers would bow down before him, certainly didn't know that he would become successful in Egypt, and even less that he needed to be sent there. He certainly went by unconventional means, for he went as a slave, not as a free man.

Despite these periods of difficulty or apparent failure, these men realised that these times did not define their lives. As I have learned, failure is not an event, but a judgement on an event. Failure is not something that happens to us or a label we put on things; it is a way of thinking about the results. For example, before Thomas Edison invented the light bulb, he failed 10,000 times. He said he had not failed but had found 10,000 ways that wouldn't work.

In the same way, Sir Edmund Hillary, after an unsuccessful attempt to scale Mount Everest, said that he was still going to beat it, because the mountain had grown all it was ever going to, but he was still growing.

If we realise this, we will enjoy the day that the Lord has made, and we will be happy in it. Let me emphasise once again the importance of living today; after all, yesterday is gone and tomorrow belongs to no one except God.

Since tomorrow and today belong to God, I will trust Him with tomorrow, but I will make the most of today, for it is a present from Him for my life.

I realise that you want to plant today to reap tomorrow, and my advice is to do just that. Plant much in order to reap much tomorrow, but rejoice today and delight yourself in today's fruit. For tomorrow that fruit will be old, just like the manna God gave the Israelites in the wilderness that had to be eaten on the day it was collected, or it would be rotten the next day. So it is with the fruits of tomorrow – they can only be enjoyed when tomorrow becomes today.

Reflection Time

The school of life is full of trials and temptations; it is also full of betrayal, disappointments and failures, but according to James 1:2-5 they have a purpose in our life:

> Consider it pure joy, my brothers and sisters, whenever you face trials of many kinds, because you know that the testing of your faith produces perseverance. Let perseverance finish its work so that you may be mature and complete, not lacking anything. If any of you lacks wisdom, you should ask God, who gives generously to all without finding fault, and it will be given to you.

It says that we will 'face trials' and situations will test our faith, but this is all with a goal to produce 'perseverance', so we will be 'mature and complete, not lacking anything'. This looks like a dream because it is all I wish for, but my wish comes without the trial and testing.

As I cannot have a rose without thorns, I may not be able to be who God wants me to be without the hardships, but He gave me two things to be a winner. He said that I should consider this a 'pure joy', as it is a fantastic opportunity for growth and, secondly, He said that He is by my side and is willing to give me wisdom, so I will be victorious over whatever area my faith is being tested in.

So now is your time to list the things you are going through, smile at them and ask God for wisdom, knowing that you will be a better person when they are over.

Chapter Nineteen
A Time for Everything

One cloudy, cold morning I sat down on some rocks in a park near my house and cried. The day before had been a disaster. It seemed like everything had gone wrong and everyone seemed to be putting demands on me. I was questioning life, telling God that it wasn't fair that we only had twenty-four hours in a day, because how could we possibly please everyone? How could I give time to my family, our friends, work and church?

That day the demands seemed to be coming from every side. My wife had called and told me she missed me, but what she was really saying was that I wasn't spending enough time with her. I was imagining what it would be like if we had children, and a terrible fear came over me: fear that I wouldn't be able to handle the time pressures. Besides my dear wife, my boss had also pressured me. I had tried to say 'no' to a last-minute request owing to other commitments, but because I felt I always had to be on call, I went into work to please my boss.

As if that weren't enough, my pastor called to tell me that we had not been giving enough time to our activities at church, and asking me why I had not been at the last leaders' meeting, which I had missed because I had been working late.

It really seemed like I wasn't fulfilling my most important obligations, much less the extra things I had added to my life, thinking they would be blessings to me and my family.

So many activities, so many things to do, so many dreams to realise, so many promises to keep, so much to believe in for the future, all without the ability to even cope with today. In the midst of all that anguish, once again I looked up to heaven and I asked God, 'How can I live my life with excellence if I can't find the time to do half the things I think I have to do?'

In my mind, I had more activities than I was able to think about right then, and they felt more like a heavy weight than productive action in the direction of my dreams.

Suddenly I remembered Ecclesiastes 3:1: 'There is a time for everything, and a season for every activity under the heavens'. I pretended not to pay attention, but the passage kept coming back to my mind. I tried to tell the Lord that when we're sad He should send us a motivational prophecy, but when that didn't work, I tried to convince God that I was just like the people of Israel, and I needed a prophet like Isaiah to cheer me up and tell me that everything was going to work out.

However, since the passage stayed in my head, I decided to argue with God about what I could do about it. After all, since He was eternal, maybe He had never had this problem with time, with the exception of His Son, Jesus. But things were different in those days: people didn't need as much time; life was much easier; there were no cars, no mobile phones and no internet, so no one could expect you to be in a particular place at a particular time.

A few days later, I opened the Bible and read all of chapter 3 of Ecclesiastes and began to feel overwhelmed again. As soon as I read the passage, that feeling, which had been dormant for a few days, woke up and started knocking at my door, and this time it brought friends with it. Now I didn't just feel like everyone around me was making demands on me; I felt like God was too; He was telling me clearly that there is time for everything, which included the situations for which I should have had time, as well as all the others that were in my head right now.

But as I was thinking these things and rebelling against God, another word came to mind – one that was very familiar to me as a student of administration – a keyword for every activity carried out in business that appears in all its materials, from the most basic to the most advanced: planning.

For all our activities, there is a plan. In some cases it is well thought out, which involves thinking in advance with considerable discernment, pondering the time and actions needed to carry it out. However, in other cases it is weak; in other words, the activity is carried out with practically no planning, for we make the decision at the last minute without taking key factors in the situation into consideration.

We can compare the first case to a driver who is going to take a trip and gets ready by consulting a map and marking out their route. That way, they feel confident that they will be going the best way possible and will get to their destination in the expected amount of time.

In the second case, without planning, even if the driver makes no mistakes en route, they can't be sure that they will arrive at their destination on time, so they forfeit the privilege of enjoying a peaceful, stress-free drive. Anything can happen if checks aren't made: a bridge could be closed, the car could run out of petrol, or any number of other mishaps might occur, making the trip less secure.

In our lives, there are many things that are supposed to happen, but we are often late seeing them fulfilled. I believe that we will always get to our destination, because as we read in Philippians 1:6, God will complete what He has begun in our lives, but I'm tired of being late and adding stress to the blessing. So then, having been reminded that there is time for everything under the sun, I look at the complexity of time and wonder why I seem to always be late. I wonder what things I can do to enable myself to live in the present in practical ways.

When we are making a cake, we need a plan, because every ingredient has its time and place in the recipe. So, when the time comes to make the cake, we have to prioritise the order in which we add the ingredients, as well as the amount of each one. If we don't, the cake will be nothing but a lump of dough. It is the same way in life, because we have to learn to prioritise so that it can take shape and have flavour, just like the cake. Prioritising is very important because it helps us define what is worth doing and what is not, and which ingredients should be part of our lives.

If we don't learn how to set priorities, we will not have time to do everything that comes up, even if the day by some miracle had more than twenty-four hours in it. Actually, we may never have the time we need to do everything we think we should, because many of those things are not only unnecessary, but they add nothing to our lives and shouldn't be there, not even in the realm of the imagination.

Due to the fact that we always have things we want to do and activities that others want us to do, we have to learn to do the most important things. I'm sure that some of you are thinking about work and putting your home and family in second place. Some of you are doing the very opposite, because all of us have values that, thanks to diversity, are different, and we can praise the Lord for that.

Who hasn't had the experience of having a number of things to do on the same day, such as two birthday parties, a church event and a wedding to go to on a Saturday, and even though we wish we could do them all, have had to choose one to the detriment of the others?

Different things will go into making that decision for different people. For example, if you were a parent of the one having a birthday, then the birthday party would be a priority for you. However, if you were the best man at the wedding, then that would become a priority for you; and if you were the worship leader that day, then the church event would be the highest priority.

C Ray Johnson, in his book, *CEO Logic: How to Think and Act Like a Chief Executive*,[73] says it like this:

> Prioritizing is the answer to the problems of time management – not computers, not efficient assistants. You don't have to work more or eliminate periods of low productivity to make better use of your time. You need to give more time to the right things.

When I look at what he said in light of my own failures and try to review my past to see where I went wrong, I can see how many times I failed to reach my goal because I prioritised the wrong things.

I have a classic example having to do with my vocation: I love to teach classes; I've discovered that I love being a teacher. I was teaching in a mission school, and everything was going well. I felt fulfilled, but a financial proposition came along that was very good for me, so I gave up my teaching career and spent the next seven years working as a chauffeur. Because I made a decision that was not conducive to my dreams, I ended up spending a number of years going in the opposite direction from the destination I wanted. During that time, I went down many unnecessary paths, and I learned a valuable lesson, namely, how to start all over again.

---

[73] C Ray Johnson, *CEO Logic: How to Think and Act Like a Chief Executive* (Wayne, NJ: Career Press, 1998, Kindle edition), location 2848 of 3021.

The first step in planning, then, is to put the highest value on what we want to attain in the long term, on what will make us feel most fulfilled.

Based on this perspective, we then begin to identify what is the highest priority at every step along the way, and consequently set short-term goals.

Once our goals are defined, we can examine each of our activities in light of those goals, whether they be at work, at home or with friends, and from this, we can make our schedule fit in with our action plan.

This is extremely important and we should learn with the Pareto principle,[74] which suggests that 20 per cent of our activity achieves most of the value –around 80 per cent. On the other hand, the rule also says that 80 per cent of our activities typically contribute to less than 20 per cent of our work value. If this observation is true, we should then place the highest value on that vital 20 per cent and focus on those activities. If we do so, we can achieve faster, greater and deeper results, which will yield a return not only in productivity and efficiency, with the resulting financial gains, but also in terms of time freed up for the other vital aspects of our life besides work, such as our family, our friends and ourselves.

We need to learn how important our family is. I remember a conversation I had with a friend while I was in seminary about how he managed to fit everything into his life. He said to me, 'When you have a family you'll realise how precious every part of your day is, and you'll learn to divide up your time wisely to reach various goals.'

---

[74] https://due.com/blog/the-pareto-principle-the-secret-of-successful-freelancers/ (accessed 24th October 2018).

Now I understand what he was saying; I don't know if I'm so good at it, but at least I can understand it. If we learn to organise our time, we can agree with Solomon: there is time for everything under the sun, except for time to waste and throw away. Please, don't get me wrong. I am not saying that there is no time to rest, to play, or to take a nap in the hammock, for rest is very important in our lives – remember that God created the world in six days and rested on the seventh, as an example to us. We have an obligation to take care of ourselves, for we are whole people; both our minds and our bodies need to be healthy, and for this we need to sleep well, eat well and have leisure time, but there is no time to waste, to go unused, without a defined purpose.

Since we're talking about planning, I would like to bring up some other things that have to do with this critical daily task. It helps us set priorities according to what is most important and take unnecessary tasks and throw them in the bin. However, we have to remember that nothing is written in stone. As time goes by, our goals can also change, for the simple reason that the world is continuously changing. So then, we need to be attentive, so as to change our priorities in each new context. We also need to stay focused on how to save time by freeing ourselves from things we can delegate or leave undone. We need to always be on the lookout for ways to build our destiny, so as to carry out the plans God has for our lives.

God's plan for our destiny cannot be frustrated, because what God has for us, no one can take away from us. But we can waste years before we allow God to bring it to pass, by constantly interrupting His work.

I'm convinced that when God told us to live an abundant life,[75] He wasn't telling us to have lots of things to do every day; He wants us to find satisfaction in everything we do. We need to find joy in all the things we do. We should make the most of every moment in our day, even in the more gruelling tasks, because they are there for one purpose – there is undoubtedly at least some pleasure and joy to be found in them. Even if I don't like my work, I can be sure that it will bring in money that provides food and fun for me and my family, so pleasure will come about as a result of what I am doing.

So, let's find joy in everything – in all of our tasks. Let's break the chains of grumbling, even in our small talk with one another, and instead let's celebrate every opportunity in our lives. This is the day that the Lord has made, so let us rejoice in every opportunity that comes our way; let us rejoice in every moment, for He is in control of everything. Our job, besides discerning our priorities, is to simply prioritise the joy and gladness in this day that the Lord has made. Hallelujah!

Reflection Time

It is time to prioritise and get balance now.

- Prioritise. You can use the 'four boxes' system to determine what is a priority for you:[76]

---

[75] See John 10:10.
[76] https://www.eisenhower.me/eisenhower-matrix/ (accessed 24th October 2018).

- o Box 1 – Urgent and important. Do it now.

- o Box 2 – Important, not urgent. Decide when to do it.

- o Box 3 – Urgent, not important. Delegate it.

- o Box 4 – Not important, not urgent. Delete it.

- Balance. Create a weekly timetable and see how you are using your time regarding the different activities and relationships you have in your life (remember that balance does not mean spending the same time but spending enough time in each area).

Chapter Twenty
Learning to Punctuate the Day

Maria Estela has just woken up. It's still early; the sun hasn't even started to come up, but she knows she has to get up. She has a lot of things to do that day—make breakfast for her husband and two daughters, take her daughters to school and go on from there to work, then come back to take the children swimming, and after getting home at the end of the day, make dinner, clean the house, put the children to bed and still get caught up on other jobs around the house and for the family.

This is Maria Estela's day, which seems very similar to that of many mothers. It also resembles the days of other people who are so busy with different responsibilities that they never stop and, in some ways, it resembles days that all of us have had. I have personally never heard anyone say that their day was peaceful, that there was no pressure to do anything, that everything fitted together perfectly and left time for other activities, or even for rest. It seems like we live in a culture of 'never enough'; and time is the main ingredient of that culture: in the morning we are usually worried about how we are going to get all our tasks done for that day, and at night, in the vast majority of cases, we complain that we didn't get everything done that we had planned.

After Adam sinned, God said that from then on, all men would eat by the sweat of their brows (Genesis 3:19); in other words, there would be no food without work. And so, we work to earn money, which is our currency of exchange, and with it we acquire food and other goods that have value to us and that we need in this modern world.

So then, since Adam, we have to work for a living, but we also work in other areas of our lives – personal, emotional and spiritual. We can't procrastinate in any of these areas because we can't put off until tomorrow what has to be done today. This creates a conflict that we have to learn how to manage, and to do that we have to learn to give priority to what is most important in our lives.

Jesus had three years to carry out His ministry and teach everything to twelve men, which is really very little time. Imagine how much pressure they would have felt to learn everything and get ready to be the pillars of the Church, if they knew they just had this short time. But how did He and His disciples manage to find time to live and still do all the things they needed to do?

Jesus set aside time to be with the Father and also to be alone with His friends. We also need to learn to do this in our lives if we are going to be able to live better.

In the midst of the daily grind, we need to remember that there is time for everything under the sun. Planning and prioritising are the rules for a better life.

In this war against time, we often blame our work for not having time for our children, but we forget how many activities we can do together if we think creatively. I'll give an example: I was camping once with some friends and their families. They wanted to go hiking with their children, but how to get them to do it? They came up with a scavenger hunt – they made a list of various objects, and whoever brought back the most items on the list would win a prize. All along the way, the children picked up objects that were on the list; in that way, they participated in the hike and had a happy time with their parents.

When you go to a church meeting, why not take the whole family along and create a time of relationship-building and spiritual growth?

We can certainly put commas in our time before it is too late to save what we are losing. For instance, we tend to forget to pause for a moment in our day to pray. We forget about God and think that we are capable of doing everything ourselves. We wake up very early, turn on the internet, drink a quick cup of coffee, because we're confident that God will bless our day – after all, He loves us – and then we do a million things. Then at night, when we're already exhausted, we remember Him, say a quick prayer and turn over to go to sleep. We forget that because He loves us, He wants to spend time with us; He wants us to be children who love to spend time with their Father.

That reminds me of the story of Martha and Mary in Luke 10: neither one of them was wrong, but Mary chose 'the better part' (verse 42, NRSV).

Great men of God have always known this and have testified that putting things in God's hands makes all the difference. Martin Luther said that the more things he had to do that day, the more time he spent in prayer. So he believed that God was in control of all things, including his day and the things he had to get done.

When we do the opposite, I think God puts a few extra missions into our day and a few details to remind us of Him. After all, He said that He is a jealous God[77] and He is jealous of us when we put other things before and above Him. I could give you a lot of advice and ideas, but you are the one who knows where you need to invest your time, put in a comma or a full stop, or get other people involved. I say this because many times we think we are the only ones who are capable of doing certain things. For example, we think that no one else can care for our children, so we can't leave them with family members or friends to have a weekend alone as husband and wife, to remind ourselves that we are, first and foremost, a couple.

This can happen at work too. We are afraid that if someone else learns how to do our job, our boss will fire us, but we forget that if we have someone helping us, we will be more productive and may even get that promotion we want so badly.

Sometimes we have to put a full stop to some activity in our lives. By this, I don't mean that we have to put an end to a dream, but sometimes we are trying to do things that aren't part of our dream, and other times we have to abandon strategies that aren't working. Peter Drucker, a famous management consultant in the 1990s, said that in order to do new things, we need to stop doing the old ones.[78] To improve the things we're already doing, we not

---

[77] See Exodus 34:14.
[78] https://www.goodreads.com/author/quotes/12008.Peter_F_Dr ucker (accessed 16th October 2018).

only have to start doing those things, but most importantly, we have to stop doing things that are not being productive, or that are keeping us from moving forward.

In a quote generally attributed to Einstein, no one can keep on doing the same things and expect to get different results.

So, I would like to challenge you to ask for wisdom to plan your life; to have times of rest and times to stop what you're doing and breathe; and wisely to make the most of the day that the Lord has made. Rejoice and be glad in the busiest days that are full of things to do, knowing that in the midst of all of them you have chosen to do the best.

Reflection Time

I just started a new course, and they were talking about the punctuation and structure of an essay and other works. Similarly, we are writing a book, which is our life. Please, be the editor of your book now and see it objectively. Help yourself, as the author, to know where you need to stop for a breath, or what you need to stop, full stop. Or maybe there is a paragraph that needs to be expanded. Now is the time!

- Where do you need to put a comma?

- To what do you need to put a full stop?

- What do you need to expand?

Chapter Twenty-one
One Day Speaks to Another

Larissa didn't wake up very early. She went into the kitchen to make breakfast, but something wasn't quite right. Moreover, she had not had a good night. She felt like a battle had taken place while she was asleep. While she was boiling water to make coffee, she remembered that she had gone to sleep angry at her boyfriend. The argument they had had late at night had been at the wrong time, at an inappropriate moment, and everything seemed confusing.

She hoped that this morning, even though it was cloudy, would be unique because it was her birthday. It was supposed to be an extraordinary day, but it seemed like the day before had told her that things were not going the way she wanted them to in her life, and the night had not succeeded in silencing the dialogue.

This happens because our minds aren't paralysed, nor do they go into a state of hibernation while we are sleeping, although their rhythm slows down. Many scholars say that our dreams are projections of things that happened during the day.

There is a verse that says, 'Each day informs the following day; each night announces to the next' (Psalm

19:2, CEV). This verse is part of a broader context, which is part of a great poem about creation and the blessings of God, but I think we can apply it here in our meditation, based on the simple fact that everything that happens to us on a given day affects us on the next. Everything we do today will have consequences tomorrow; in other words, whatever we sow today we will reap tomorrow.

When we live today in the best way possible, we are sowing a better future, but if we sow a lousy day today, tomorrow we will reap a bad day. Of course, we need to remember that we can only live one day at a time, but it's essential that we rewrite our past and write our future.

So then, tomorrow we will wake up in the reality we sowed today, and tomorrow will be our new today, and our today will be tomorrow's yesterday. So, let's make sure that each cycle goes around in the best way possible so that the next cycle begins full of the best things. We need to establish a cycle that begins and ends every twenty-four hours and determine how to end one day and begin the next.

The Bible tells us that 'the days are evil' (see Ephesians 5:16). When Paul wrote this, inspired by the Holy Spirit, he was bearing witness to something we already know by experience. We face various situations during the day that can frustrate us and make us angry, but Paul also tells us that we need to get rid of our anger before the sun goes down (see Ephesians 4:26). We need to leave it in today, for tomorrow will be another day, and we shouldn't take it with us. We can get angry, but we need to be careful not to sin or carry our anger into the following day.

Even if it seems difficult to leave our problems or our anger behind, we need to experience the delight of accepting the truth that God takes care of us. We need to realise that these words of Jesus are real every day of our lives: 'Come to me, all you who are weary and burdened, and I will give you rest' (Matthew 11:28).

In Psalm 68:19 it is written: 'Praise be to the Lord, to God our Saviour, who daily bears our burdens.' We should visualise our burdens every day, put them in God's hands and have confidence that He hears our prayers and requests. That way, we can actually envision good things and keep our brains occupied with them instead. We can sleep peacefully, without carrying anything terrible into the following day, because we have left everything that weighed us down in God's hands. I can guarantee that there is no one better able to deal with these things.

Besides ending the daily cycle well, we need to begin it well so that we can have a good day and another good ending. The Word tells us: 'Weeping may endure for a night, But [the] joy [of the Lord] comes in the morning' (see Psalm 30:5, NKJV). We have to believe that in every new cycle God has new things in store for us.

One of the reasons we can believe this promise is that the mercies of the Lord are 'new every morning' (see Lamentations 3:23), so His love, which never ends and never fails, brings us a new promise every day: that anything we did yesterday that was wrong has been forgotten by God and that now He has something new for us.

If joy has been renewed, if mercies have been renewed, if our account with another 86,400 seconds has been reopened, then what perspective are we going to take on the day: that of someone who is counting down the time to their release from prison, or that of someone who has found a hidden treasure?

Remember what the Lord says in Isaiah 55:8-9:

> For my thoughts are not your thoughts, neither are your ways my ways ... As the heavens are higher than the earth, so are my ways higher than your ways and my thoughts than your thoughts.

So, we can be sure that God has more in store for us than we can imagine.

For this reason, God has also given us a strategy for daily life. Jesus tells us that in order to have a wonderful day and a victorious life we have to 'seek first his kingdom', and all the things we need will also be given to us (Matthew 6:33).

The Word calls us to proclaim the salvation of God every day. Of course, we are to proclaim it to 'all nations', for that is the commission that was given to us by Jesus in Matthew 28:19-20, but Psalm 96 goes beyond that. The psalmist tells us to 'Declare his glory' and the marvellous things He has done every day, what He has done for His people and wants to do for everyone: 'Sing to the LORD, praise his name; proclaim his salvation day after day' (verse 2). But how can I proclaim in the morning the great things God has done if I have gone through nothing but problems? The truth is that when we see only problems, our focus is not on God and we start to live like men and women of little faith. We'll always be ungrateful that way because we don't see what God has done in our lives, beginning with the fact that we are alive, among other things, and because we don't believe that He will add to us[79] all the things we need.

So then, remember that God is with you in the small daily things and that He is with you also in the big things. When the bigger tasks with a certain degree of difficulty come along, remember that you are not alone. You have friends by your side; you have the body of Christ – other believers – to share your problems. And above all, you have the Almighty God, for whom nothing is impossible. If God is on our side, the Word confirms that 'I can do [everything] through him who gives me strength' (Philippians 4:13).

End your day well; resolve your problems; put everything in God's hands. One day speaks to another, and if we sleep poorly, we will tend to wake up badly, but if the sun does not set on our anger and we sleep well, we will wake up well. And if you don't sleep well, when you wake up, repeat the Bible verse quoted in this chapter, that the mercies of God are 'new every morning'. Remembering the good things the Lord has done can give us hope that in God we can do all things, and if we have good plans, He has even better plans for our lives and our days.

In this chapter, we have seen how important the beginnings and endings of our days are. So, I would like to ask you to spend ten minutes when you wake up and before you go to sleep thinking about happy things.

As Tommy Newberry says, we need to programme our mental software to be joyful throughout the day. Like a

---

[79] See Matthew 6:33, NKJV.

child on the night before Christmas, who wakes up excited about opening their presents, we need to programme ourselves to expect that it will be a good day and that we will be joyful in it, for this new day is a gift from God to us.

What you do with these first and last ten minutes is up to you and depends on what you are experiencing in your life. I remember waking up and spending the first ten minutes listening to music with inspiring lyrics on YouTube, or using that time to pray. I know of people who stand in front of the mirror and say, 'How much joy you have today is up to you.' Think about three good things, or at least one, and start making this your morning and evening ritual of joy.[80]

In closing, I want to make one more point.

After Jesus rose from the dead, He appeared a number of times to His disciples and one of those times He told them that they would be baptised with the Holy Spirit 'in a few days'.[81] So, they asked Him if that would be the time that He would restore the kingdom of Israel. Jesus answered that it was not for people to know the hour and the time. From this response, it is clear to me that it is not for us to know the future or live in the past, but to live decisively right now, which is the time the Lord gives us.

All the same, when the disciples received the Holy Spirit, everything changed. Their view of the kingdom of God changed, and they saw that there was only one moment in which they could live – right now. With this new way of looking at the world, and filled with the power of God, they went out to tell the world who Jesus was. They

---

[80] Newberry, *The 4:8 Principle*, pp145-147.
[81] Acts 1:5.

put their lives on the line, as they began to understand that God and His Spirit were much more important than anything else, more important than their simple past and much more important than their future here on earth, for now, they had the certainty of heaven.

Let me remind you right now, son or daughter of God, that you are empowered by the Holy Spirit to have a full life – full of good thoughts, full of colours – for the One who transformed the apostles is changing your life and will change it even more, to the degree that you allow Him to work.

I invite you to live in the daily fullness of a God who made this day for you, so you can rejoice and be glad in it.

Reflection Time

Someone once said that knowledge is power,[82] but I discovered later that this is not precisely true, because knowledge without action is only potential power, while the action is the power being used.

• So, now is time to think about your Morning Ritual and your Evening Ritual. How might you start them – with prayer or listening to music? List some ideas below:

---

[82] Generally attributed to Sir Francis Bacon.

Chapter Twenty-two

Ready to Live Today to the Fullest

We come now to the final chapter. I hope that this has been a journey of learning how to make the most of today, and to enjoy nothing less than the now that God has given us, for this day is a present from Him.

The mercies and the love of God are new every morning, and I hope that your desire to have a close relationship with Him has also been renewed. As a result, the quality of your life, your actions and your relationships will be better. Maybe what I'm about to say now should have been put at the beginning of the book, but I am including it here as a final exhortation to go through life counting all your days.

Remember that we only learn to count our days if we live fully in them because if we don't, we will not have really lived.

We have looked at various principles throughout the book: how to stop living in the past; how to give our anxiety about the future to God, who is the only one the future belongs to; that there are difficult days and days of victory. I want to leave with you two verses from the apostle Paul to help us live out everything that has been said. The first one is:

> We know that in all things God works for the good of those who love him, who have been called according to his purpose.
> *Romans 8:28*

Whether our days are easy or difficult, we need to understand that they are all pieces in a giant puzzle. When I was a child, I helped my sister put together a 10,000-piece puzzle. Some of the pieces were easy to place because they had distinctive patterns; others were only one colour and looked like they could go anywhere. Some of them were beautiful with pretty shapes; others didn't seem to have any logic to them and didn't appear to fit anywhere. But in the end, they all worked together to form a beautiful landscape. And just like every piece worked together to create a whole, so all our days work together to build a life.

Who wouldn't say that Joseph, son of Jacob, had the dream job, with all that power in his hands? But if we just looked at all the individual episodes of his life, who would say that they were building a pretty picture? The things he went through, including losing contact with his family, being sold as a slave, and working in prison, don't seem to create a story of forgiveness, love, overcoming, salvation and, above all, the fulfilment of a dream.

The second verse is:

> I have learned the secret of being content in any and every situation.
> *Philippians 4:12*

This verse shows us the basis on which we can learn to count our days and live happy lives. When I came to London, I got a job as a chauffeur, and in the contract I signed there was a clause saying that I couldn't have any other job because I had to be available whenever I was called. So I started to work a lot of Sundays and miss church services, small group meetings and leadership meetings. The whole time I was deeply anxious, wanting to get a different job.

One day someone told me I couldn't go on that way. I had to see that God was in control of everything. So, if He was allowing me to have that job, what could I do? I thought about this and the following week I made a plan: I made a promise to God that I would give an extra 10 per cent of my income to Him as an offering; in other words, in addition to the tithe I would give another 10 per cent. I hoped He would help me to stop working inappropriate hours.

Funnily enough, nothing changed, so I carried on missing church meetings because of work, but I learned that even when God says 'no' to our prayer, He is still being God, and if He was allowing me to work this schedule, He must have a plan.

I came to see that He has a plan when He moves the mountain before me and when He doesn't move it. He guides me with His 'yes' and also with His 'no'.

I then focused on the fact that I should be content in every single circumstance, asking God for strength to say, 'It is Well with My Soul'. This is the title of a hymn written by Horatio Gates Spafford.[83] Spafford was born on 20th October 1828 in Troy, Rensselaer County in New York, USA. In 1861 he married a young woman call Anna Larsen, in Chicago. They were friends of the great evangelist Dwight L Moody. Spafford was a successful lawyer, but lost considerable assets in the Great Fire of Chicago in 1871. They also lost a son, who died of scarlet fever at the age of four. Then in 1873 Spafford and his wife decided to go on holiday to England, where Moody was preaching. But due to business commitments, Spafford didn't join his wife and four young daughters on the *SS Ville du Havre*. He sent them on ahead, planning to join them later. But there was a collision with another ship and 226 people died. Anna Spafford survived, but their children were all lost. Anna sent her husband a telegram saying, 'Saved alone'.

Spafford made the journey to England, journeying near the place where his daughters had lost their lives. Consequently, he wrote the hymn 'It is Well with My Soul' with its deeply touching lyrics.

This beautiful song was written in a time of great pain but also when a man who had suffered greatly could feel the peace that is above all human understanding that only Christ can give. What a tragic history; one never forgotten, although the Spaffords went on to have more children.

As for me, some years later, God decided to move the mountain. I changed my job, and my new position came with a lot of perks. But the best thing was what I learned from that period – perseverance. As a consequence, I am more complete as a person than I was before.

---

[83] 1828–88.

By learning to give thanks in all situations – in want or in abundance, in joy or in sorrow – and to rejoice and be glad at all times and on all days, we will learn to count our days and, as a result, we will gain a heart of wisdom. When we have a wise heart, we will know how to make the best use of our days; and when we make the best use of our days, they will be happy ones. That is my wish for you.

Don't forget: yesterday is over, tomorrow has not yet come, and today is a present from God.

I'm sure you have received many presents in your life. All of them had something special for you inside, but some of them came wrapped in packages that were harder to open than others. So it is with our days. Every one is a present delivered by God, when 86,400 new seconds are deposited into our account. Some of them seem more complicated than others to deal with but, like all presents, they come for the purpose of making us rejoice and be glad, so we can avail ourselves of the abundance He has planned for us.

> For I know the thoughts that I think toward you,
> says the LORD, thoughts of peace and not of evil,
> to give you a future and a hope.
> *Jeremiah 29:11 (NKJV)*

It is not for us to know the future or live in the past; the only time that God has given us to live in is now.

So, in closing, I invite you to live today and every day to the fullest, in the extravagant generosity of a God who made this day so that you could rejoice and be glad in it.

Reflection Time

- As a reward for finishing this book, celebrate with someone this new moment in your life, and live it to the fullest!

  The Lord bless you
  and keep you;
  the Lord make his face shine on you
  and be gracious to you;
  the Lord turn his face toward you
  and give you peace"